FEARLESS COLD CALLING

How to Turn Cold Leads
into Hot Prospects

Mark Sanford, Ph.D.

Montaigne Publishing

Orinda, California

Library of Congress Control Number: 2001119089

First Printing October 2001

Second Printing April 2002

Third Printing July 2003

ISBN: 0-917430-30-1

TABLE OF CONTENTS

PREFACE

I have a good friend who has been divorced for over a year, but still can't bring herself to go to a singles group. She says it's too demeaning. Betty Ford, queen of the recovery movement, says that for the longest time she couldn't speak up in AA meetings. She thought they would laugh at her. My wife Deborah just can't say no to telemarketers. She doesn't want to hurt their feelings.

At one time or another, we are all faced with a situation where we know what the right response is, but we just can't seem to say or do it. Something holds us back. Instead of taking pride in an outcome, we end up suffering the pain of guilt and self-recrimination for failing to follow our own best-laid plans. These failures of will can take a variety of forms. For me it was an inability to make telephone cold calls to build my business. For others, it might take the form of fear of public speaking, stage fright, or the simple unwillingness to ask someone for a date.

My first encounter with "avoidance" took place when I was a teenager living on a 30-acre farm near Poughkeepsie, New York. One autumn morning, some deer hunters came across our property. My mother directed my older brother Michael and me to chase them off. Michael hung back (he was more shy than I was!) while I bravely trudged forward toward the well-armed party of hunters. From a safe distance of 200 yards I roared, "Get off the property! Can't you see it's posted?" Quietly, they retreated into the woods and left our land.

I didn't realize it at the time but this contact had two of the fundamental features of a cold call: the approach was un-expected and the poachers/prospects were unknown to me.

The lesson I took away from that day was that approaching strangers is not easy for everyone (witness my older and bigger brother's avoidance) but if you can do it, it can make you feel quite powerful!

The chapters that follow are designed to share with you what I have learned in my career. It is the story of how I overcame call avoidance; the techniques I developed to help others overcome it; and a simple system I've developed that will help you earn the income you deserve.

1. My Humble Beginnings

Because I've had a lot of success in telephone sales and in teaching others how to do the same, almost everyone seems to believe that it has always been that way for me. On the contrary, my beginnings in cold calling, both in person and on the telephone, were less than stellar. In fact, they were horrible.

I began my career in real estate sales in the early 1980's and was hired at an Oakland, California Century 21 office. I fell into residential sales because the training time was short, the initial investment was minimal and it was easy to find a job.

The year I started, interest rates were 18% and the market was extremely slow. My sales manager, Joe Murray, told me to get out of the office and introduce myself to homeowners. The prospect of calling on total strangers filled me with dread. I was shy to the point of actual trembling. The only thing I was sure of at the time was that no one was buying homes!

I'd recently had a good job as an administrator at a small graduate school, the Wright Institute in Berkeley, but was sent packing when budget cuts slashed staff positions. With a wife and three sons under age 13 (Craig, Nate and Colin), I needed to bring in some money. My wife worked part time as a teacher's aide, but earned only $6,000 a year. I detested the idea that I couldn't support the family. I could not accept that my wife was supporting me. It was ego deflating. So the pressure was on to produce.

In the office in the Montclair district, a middle class enclave in the Oakland Hills, there were about 15 full-time agents, including my new friends Harry Barnfather and Herb Master. They wouldn't make cold calls; they claimed it was a waste of time. But Joe, my sales manager, convinced me that the unsolicited reaching out to strangers was a good way to bring in business. His favorite greeting was "Ya got anything for me?"

Unfortunately, the only thing I "got" instead was a prolonged inner conflict, a spiritual battle between me and my better self. The voice of conscience that told me to get out there and make those cold calls fought with my inner critic that warned against the imagined dangers of presenting myself unannounced to total strangers.

The first time out, I drove up to Bonita Street in my 1969 two-door, gray Volvo and parked. There I sat unable to move. I tried to move my hand toward the door handle, but I was frozen to the spot. I felt like I was in the grip of an invisible force.

Gradually, I was able to move and walk down the street but, I turned and marched back to the car, acting as if I were lost, in case anyone was observing me.

I am a big guy, six feet three, and 235 pounds. On my first approach to a house, my mouth was dry, my heart was pounding and my chest was tight with apprehension. I tried a door where I hoped no one was home. I knocked gently hoping no one would hear. My inner critic kept blasting me with these unanswerable admonitions "What if they say no... You'll only get rejected... Nobody likes door to door salesmen... They are the lowest of the low... They'll just slam the door in your face... The market is bad now, so it's futile to try." And I also kept hearing my own mother's words from the past... "It [sales] is beneath your dignity."

Nevertheless, I pressed on. After six tries, I finally found an elderly lady willing to talk. She answered the door on the second ring: "Yes?" she asked. I was speechless! I couldn't ask her if she wanted to sell, that was too forward. I couldn't ask her if she wanted to buy a house for clearly she already had one. I opened my mouth and said "Aaaaaaggggggh... Hi... How... I just want..." I was so embarrassed! It seemed silly and futile to just introduce myself as a local Century 21 agent. I handed her my card and mumbled something about how I was just passing through her neighborhood and wanted to introduce myself. I shuffled away feeling very foolish. I was too shy.

Back at the office, Herb and Harry didn't offer me much sympathy. Herb asked, "Well, Mark, how did you do?" "Not so hot," I answered. "This cold call stuff is hard." Harry then advised, "You ought to do like us. Hold lots of open houses and let 'em come to you. You get lots of leads off the Sunday lookers, and eventually you make sales that way." Herb added, "Right, that way you get leads, but you don't get rejected." Defending my new position, I responded, "Yes, but how many of those leads end up as sales? Or new listings?" Their only response was silence.

That evening after I got home, my wife Deborah asked "Well, how did things go?" "Oh, I gave out a few cards." Which was a lie. I gave out only one, but I wasn't going to tell her that. To be criticized on top of feeling like such a wimp would have been too much. Forcing myself to do what I didn't want to do (but felt I SHOULD do) and then failing made me discouraged and ashamed for being so cowardly. Meanwhile the bills were piling up at home. I couldn't run away. I would tell myself: "Mark, how can you be such a wimp that you can't even knock on a few doors and ask for business? You're no good for being so weak! And you don't even know why."

The next afternoon I went up to Virginia Street thinking that a different neighborhood might be less forbidding. I was sitting in the Volvo again, trying to make myself open the door when a police car pulled up alongside. The officer got out of his patrol car, came over to my side and knocked on my window. I let it down a crack and he said, "I'm sorry sir, but we received a call from someone that you were on the street acting suspiciously." Me: "Well, officer, I'm just out here calling on homeowners." Officer: "Well, you'd better move on." This was ridiculous! Here I was trying to do my job, failing at it, and being rousted from the neighborhood for loitering! That was enough to cause me to take a break from the rigors of cold calling for several weeks. (The first of many escapes). I needed time to think. I kept a journal of my thoughts at the time. Here is a sample of what I wrote:

> Cold call avoidance is an experience of anxiety followed
> by guilt. For the neophyte, the feeling is one of sullen
> suffering, and apprehension, and the origins of these
> feelings seem a mystery. Everyone knows cold calling is
> painful but supportable because it is believed to lead to

more prospects and greater profit. This activity is beneath my dignity. Door knocking, I tell myself, is degrading. You are perceived as pitiful for having to stoop so low to make a buck. I hate this. I don't like it because you make an unsolicited invasion of peoples' right to privacy.

I came to realize that thinking about cold calling instead of doing something about it was in itself an escape from a fundamental fear I didn't want to face... the fear of approaching people without an introduction. This fear was the major cause of my resistance to cold calling. I returned to the calling efforts with renewed resolve and a determination to persevere.

Three months and about 100 contacts later, I got to the point where I could put on quite a nice little speech when I was lucky enough to find a prospect. Gradually I felt more comfortable about what I would say:

Good afternoon. I just happened to be in your neighborhood and wanted to introduce myself. My name is Mark Sanford [at this point I would whip out my business card] and I am your local Century 21 agent. We offer free home appraisals to our customers and I would be more than happy to give you a free, no obligation appraisal. Would this evening or tomorrow afternoon at 2:00 be most convenient?

Sometimes it was actually fun. One time I got invited into the living room to chat with the homeowner. She was a recently widowed woman who took a shine to me. She ended up offering me a glass of wine at 2:00 in the afternoon and it began to look like more relaxation was in the offing. Out of good sense and loyalty to Deborah, I refused and managed to get out of there before doing anything I would regret. Apparently I was becoming less shy.

The number of contacts gradually increased as I discovered that my fear of giving offense was in fact groundless. For the most part, the unwritten rules of politeness protect you from others' rudeness. Even so, I found cold calling very difficult. It only became easier after hours of practice and a corresponding lessening of groundless fears.

After leaving real estate due to poor market conditions and a waning interest in the work, I took on a job of cold calling small businesses coast to coast out of the yellow pages. This was to promote pre-paid legal plans. The job site was a home office in

Walnut Creek. There was a group of callers, all using the same scripts and calling on the same kinds of businesses: dry cleaners, printers, restaurants, gas stations, beauty parlors, and so forth. I hated it. Each morning, while driving to work, my chest constricted just in anticipation of the four hours of calling I had to do. My dread was obvious and would only decrease after I began calling for a while. But getting started was the hard part. Between the dread and picking up the phone, there was a constant chatter of self-talk that was critical and self-berating. I got so sick of it that I picked up the phone for relief. And it seemed that the surroundings helped too. To be in the company of other callers made it seem less threatening; they didn't appear to bear any obvious scars from the activity.

My supervisor, Bob, was infinitely patient with me. I managed to take up lots of his time going over the fine points of handling objections as a way to avoid getting on the phone. Bob introduced me to the rhetoric of striving and success talk, which seems to go hand-in-hand with anyone who seeks to coach people to do adverse work. I was deluged with Bob's motivational rants that were all designed to get me to work longer and harder. Eventually, I worked my way up to 100 calls a day.

Getting started is recognized as the hardest part of cold calling. Once you are "in the activity" it is easier to continue. However, the inner dialogue or self-talk that gets generated before initiating these contacts is the slippery slope of the work. It's hard to put your finger on exactly what these thoughts are. Often there is a feeling of frozen constriction and dread that even today I sometimes experience when picking up the phone for an out of the blue call. It's just that now I have learned to discount and disengage from the part of myself that dislikes making contact with strangers.

After telemarketing for prepaid legal plans it was on to residential home improvement sales, working for an independent contractor installing energy conservation materials and devices in concert with the Pacific Gas and Electric Company. This was my first sustained introduction to in-person, face-to-face cold calls, knocking on doors in residential neighborhoods. I would go out at about 4:30 in the afternoon in so-called safe neighborhoods in Alameda and Contra Costa County, California. This was grueling work with lots of rejection, leavened by the occasional "lay down" as it was called when the prospect would immediately light up in eagerness at the offer and invite you in to sign a contract. This didn't happen very often but it did serve to keep me motivated.

I hated the work. But I believed in the concept of energy conservation, just as I had in the idea of property ownership and prepaid legal plans. It just seemed that the pain that had to be endured in the cold approach to enact these offers was not worth the reward.

My time in residential sales was followed by aluminum siding sales, encyclopedia sales, and network marketing forays until I finally landed back in school. This was because I became curious about what happens to those who have similar kinds of struggles, but in an entirely different arena. I particularly wondered about those people who must restrain themselves from doing what they very much want to do, such as drug addicts and alcoholics.

Not yet achieving great success in sales, I thought that converting myself into a drug counselor would be a good alternative career and would allow me to continue my explorations into self-discipline, inhibition and self motivation. I signed on for a certificate program in addiction studies at a local university and soon found myself embroiled in the world of Alcoholics Anonymous, 12 step programs, recidivism, and self-esteem. In short, I moved on to another world of strivers who instead of battling to overcome their fears and doubts, battled to conquer their cravings and temptations. Instead of forcing themselves to do what they did not want to do, addicts and alcoholics struggled to not do what they very much wanted to do.

I obtained an internship at a local treatment center that pursued the medical model of recovery at Mt. Diablo Medical Center in Concord, California. Their philosophy was that control of addiction depended first upon labeling addiction as a disease. This implied that you were powerless to fix yourself, that you needed the help of a professional healer who would guide you to recovery via the discipline of abstinence. Abstinence was the "cure" of the disease.

The difficulty was achieving abstinence over the long term. Hence the concept that the addict or alcoholic is always recovering, not recovered. Group membership in AA was the mainstay of this effort. The method by which this effort was carried forward was self-disclosure in front of a support group. You were to share what troubled you, how you had arranged your environment to reduce temptation, how you had reduced stress in your life as a way to gain control over your addiction. What interested me from a cold calling point of view was the idea that fear and self-doubt, the twin demons of every cold caller, could also be overcome by self-disclosure to others.

After about a year and a half of counseling the victims of substance abuse, it became clear to me that the problem was relapse, or as it was described in the behavioral science literature, "self regulatory failure." It also became clear that the best way to help others with this problem was to provide ways to boost self-esteem, to help people develop enough self-appreciation and self-validation that they would no longer abuse themselves. This was easier said than done.

I applied for a grant through the hospital to support this approach, but unfortunately the grant was not approved. Ultimately, I left my position at Mt. Diablo. I began offering public seminars on relapse prevention, called the LETS (Life Enhancement Training Seminar) program, but the income generated was not enough to make it worth my time. So here I was in 1992 with a precarious hold on my own self-regulatory failures, still trying to control my own fear and self-doubt in prospecting for new clients.

I returned to an outplacement group called Forty Plus in Oakland intent on finding a real job. While undergoing socialization to this organization, helping others and being helped in the job search, I ran into Mike McKay, an accountant, who was looking for new job in his chosen profession. One day I overheard him complaining about his difficulties making cold calls in the job search. I approached Mike and told him I had some expertise in this area and he responded: "Really? You could start a business helping people do that." So was launched my present successful business that focuses on helping people overcome call avoidance and expand their customer base.

2. Approaching Prospects

Direct selling and calling activity both involve crossing the social gulf that separates each of us from those who are unknown to us. In my early days of cold calling as a real estate agent, the thing that really got to me was the sheer awkwardness of approaching people I didn't know. It took me years to get over this awkwardness. Since then, I have learned it is a very common feeling among cold callers.

I remember how hard it was to get to know people in graduate school at UC Berkeley. Without being a member of a group, there were few ways to meet or approach people even though there were thousands of young people just like me surrounding me every day. I recall having the impulse to want to meet someone I found attractive or approachable, but it was always a big effort to do so. I suppose this is why dating services have been so successful over the years. They help take care of your misgivings about making the first move!

When I got into real estate and discovered how hard it was to make cold calls, it seemed like I was going through the same difficulty all over again. Not having a context for meeting people makes it difficult to strike up a conversation. Even if you are in close proximity to someone, without a common interest, membership, or experience that you both can relate to, it's hard for most people to initiate a conversation. (Not impossible, but difficult!) I could introduce myself to strangers as a realtor at open houses, but that was only because I was in the role of host that included the expectation of a self-introduction. In sales (where there is a premium on making contact one on one), there is no way around having to have an "approach," especially one you are comfortable with. Yet, with all of the prospects you are forced to contact to get to the few buyers, it can be a daunting task. For a long time, both in real estate and later in home improvement sales, I made my approach by door-to-door, or face-to-face prospecting.

Later on, I found businesses much easier to approach just by phone alone. In my mind, they were open for business from 9:00 to 5:00 and that included being ready to receive solicitations from vendors who might have an offering that would increase revenues or cut costs. In other words, they were used to being approached for business purposes. And, needless to say, phone prospecting is far more efficient than face to face prospecting in terms of numbers of contacts that can be potentially converted to qualfied leads.

My point of view was that I would feel more comfortable approaching strangers on the phone when those strangers were business prospects. But with homeowners, whether approaching them face-to-face or over the phone, there is no agreed upon "unwritten rule" that such approaches are "OK." I felt like more of an outlaw with homeowners, unless I approached them door-to-door. Even then I didn't feel great about it. But at the same time there was something challenging about it and satisfying when it led to a sale. You had the satisfaction of knowing you had overcome your fears and had successfully negotiated the sale.

After my all too brief career in real estate I switched to another form of direct selling, home improvement sales. I landed there after short sojourns into encyclopedia sales and aluminum siding sales that I also found unsuitable. Selling the Encyclopedia Britannica put more pressure on my slim sales skills than they could bear, and I didn't much care for their foot in the door techniques such as the offer of free books in exchange for an interview. To me this always felt as if you were approaching people under false pretenses. Prospects often just wanted the free books and could have cared less about making a purchase. And beside, it's really a form of bribery. To get the interview you are resorting to a play on the greed of your prospect. In doing this, you run the risk of including non-prospects. I would rather just qualify the prospect first so when I go on the interview at least I know there is genuine interest.

Aluminum siding was a different story, but also I found it troublesome on moral grounds. My mentor's big push was to get the prospect to accept him as a friend first and then hit him with the pitch. The theory was that after making a fast friend, it wouldn't really matter what you sold him. He would buy so as not to offend you.

Selling energy conservation products such as ceiling insulation and weather stripping was more to my liking. The local utility company was offering zero interest loans to homeowners and the pitch was that once you installed, the savings off your gas bill would cover the payments. We didn't have to make cold calls; we just called on people who were already qualified by our telemarketers in the home office. All we had to do was sell the deal to prospects who had already agreed to see somebody. For the most part, this worked. I felt okay about this proposition and spent the next couple of years crawling around people's attics, falling off roofs, and generally getting better at door-to-door sales work.

Despite some success with these "warm" prospects, I still had much avoidance in making cold calls to complete strangers. I now realize that simply approaching a stranger is not what makes cold calls so tough for most people. We approach all kinds of strangers every day in business situations: bank tellers, postal employees, waitpersons, store clerks, etc. Approaching these people is relatively easy because they have what you want, and they are unlikely to refuse your request since they are paid to provide it.

Creating a Pretext

In sales, there is no open invitation, you don't necessarily know the person, and you have no introduction. Think of all the strangers who live close to you in your neighborhood, whom you pass on the street every day, whom you will never connect with because you have no cover, no pretext, no reason to interact or communicate with them. What you do have to do in sales is to talk to strangers and that is precisely what causes so much anxiety.

I have a friend, Jay Wallace, who is an unemployed engineer. He enjoys visiting the local retail establishments in his community in order to strike up conversations with managers and clerks to pass the time. He does this to market himself by "wandering around." He loves meeting people in public places. Crossing the social gulf is easy for him. He sees people being available in shops and behind counters as a positive advantage for him. It makes his favorite pastime that much more easily achieved. Jay says, "I just go in, and strike up a conversation, but sometimes I think they want me to leave cause they have real customers to attend. I don't mind, because it's a great way to pass the time, and if they don't want me around, they can tell me." Unfortunately, it's not that easy for most of us.

Historically, one way salespeople have avoided this problem in business has been via third party introductions. Early in my career as a consultant and trainer I attended endless leads group meetings, Chamber of Commerce gatherings, and trade shows. My goal was to meet someone from whom I could get a business card so that when I later approached a prospect unknown to me I could use the name on the card as a reference. The idea is to ease the approach so that you will feel more comfortable in calling on an unknown prospect.

Then, when you approach the acquaintance of the person from whom you have received a card, you are better armed. Now you have a "cover" or a pretext for the call. You can say to the prospect,"Mr. Jones told me to call you." This type of approach is easier to make. You can approach this associate with less avoidance because you can use Mr. Jones' name as an introduction. You are "off the hook," so to speak, psychologically because someone else told you to call. You expect that his reception will be cordial out of his obligation to Mr. Jones even though he may not remember who "Mr. Jones" is!

When you think about it, you even need a reason to contact close friends and associates. I have a neighbor I have known for years. When she drops by, she will say, "Oh, I was out walking and needed to use your bathroom." Actually she just wants to visit. Or she'll come by with some strange fruit and say something like, "Here, I don't want this, do you want some?" It's just a pretext, an excuse for the approach, a cover that is used to save appearances, to make it seem as if what is about to happen has a utilitarian purpose to legitimate what is really just a friendly, sociable encounter.

Similarly in sales, and cold calling in particular, you need a pretext for your call. And if you don't have one, make one up! For example, "I sent you an e- mail a few days ago about... and I'm just following up." You don't care if they remember the missive or pre-call initiative. You just want an excuse to follow up. This is often the rationale behind sending out brochures and flyers; it doesn't really matter if the prospect has seen what you've sent as long as you can use it for a pretext. It helps earn you the right to make the contact and makes your call a lot easier.

3. Understanding Your "Emotional Labor"

A crossing (crossing the social gulf) made for the purpose of requesting business from a stranger is hard for most people. This is because the contact is often unwelcome, leading to a feeling of failure or rejection. That's because rejection and failure are the most likely outcomes! And, even more important, this process is likely to generate negative emotions like self-doubt, humiliation, shame or discouragement. These negative feelings must be managed in order to overcome call avoidance. Think of them as sort of a psychological cost of doing business that will eventually provide a real rate of economic return.

Here are some notes from my journal documenting my difficulty crossing the social gulf as a salesman.

> I remember wondering... Will this prospect I'm about to approach be mad at me if I call them? Will they think I am rude for interrupting whatever they are doing at that moment? Do I care? Of course I care... I hate the idea of others thinking I am a rude or impertinent person. It makes me feel guilty for being such a rube. Bugging people with what they don't want... Ugh! But, I have a right to make a living this way, and what I am offering... [energy saving conservation measures] is a good thing, and is good for them! Yet still there is a part of me that

hates this activity… making myself into an outlaw in social space, an intruder, a troublemaker. And this prospect isn't going to buy from me. He's probably already been approached by someone else anyway.

In my seminar business I have come across many professional salesfolk who dread making the first contact to find a prospect. Take Fred Jones, insurance agent from the Firemen's Fund:

> Every morning between 10:00 and 12:00 noon I try to make fifty calls to new clients… but let me tell you, it's tough work… either they aren't there and they put you into voice mail, which I hate cause they don't return my calls; or they don't want to talk to me, or they are already covered. It feels so futile sometimes… I hate it.

Trapped by False Ideas

Much of the tension around calling strangers comes from the fears you may have about their probable reaction. These thoughts are hypotheses about what you think is likely to happen. For example, the prospect will not be there; the prospect will not be interested; the prospect will be offended that you called; the prospect has already received lots of calls from your competitors; or you will be terribly unhappy when the prospect turns you down.

These are typical predictions about what is likely to happen if you call. But typically, unlike what normally happens with a hypothesis, they don't get tested. Rather, the prediction becomes itself a reason not to call, even though it may be totally false!

Based on years of calling for various marketing propositions, it is my conviction that telephone prospectors are often trapped by false ideas about how they will be perceived by the prospect. They think their predictions are real or true, based on very slim evidence. Hence they act on them, or rather fail to act on them, and don't know that they are in fact false. They are immobilized or frozen by the false idea that precludes getting feedback from the real world. Without feedback to modify their constructs, they hang on to their false ideas and never make the calls. Over the years, I have come to believe that most call avoidance is mainly caused by these negative predictions that are untested and hence block the calling activity.

I know a real estate agent who was sure that calling in the evening would always get her a rude reception. When I convinced her to call anyway and test this idea, she found that instead most people treated her with respect. A burglar alarm salesperson hated the idea of approaching strangers without a referral because he was sure that any prospect had been approached thousands of times already by the competition, and therefore it was futile. When I encouraged him to try anyway (and keep careful records), he discovered that while many had been approached, a healthy percentage were ready to buy because all the sales activity indicated that this must be a hot item! A financial planner hated making calls because he was convinced that too much telemarketing had polluted the environment. He was sure people were sick of receiving so many calls. But after testing the waters by calling only small business people, he found that this wasn't true at all. In fact, he regularly made six appointments for every 40 contacts with his prospect base.

It is these false ideas and predictions that often cause call avoidance. And because we tend to believe them, we become trapped and victimized by negative thoughts that cost us the money we deserve to earn!

Overcoming the Mysterious Force of Nameless Dread

The mysterious sensation of nameless dread as one comes close to making the call is often compounded by not being able to identify what it is within oneself that triggers this negative feeling. All one knows is that something is operating outside of awareness that has got you in its grip.

Here's what Tom Waters once said about it:

> Sometimes when I called I got this feeling of a cold clammy fist tightening around the middle of my chest. I wanted to pick up the phone but I just couldn't. My nervousness was visceral and I had to get up and walk around. I'd find anything else to do just to avoid having to make that call. And the thing is, I didn't understand why I felt that way; I mean, it was no big deal if they say 'no' and I don't even know these people! Nevertheless, sometimes I just can't make that call.

To be successful as a cold caller or telephone prospector, it is necessary to manage these negative thoughts and emotions. Actually, this is what constitutes the "work" in this type of labor. Arlie Hochschild in her book *The Managed Heart* (University of California Press, 1983) coined the term "emotional labor." This is labor that requires us to suppress certain feelings in order to create an appearance that produces the proper state of mind in others. In the case of cold calling, the challenge is to create in the prospect's mind the conviction that one is a trustworthy vendor of a needed good or service. The last thing we want to convey is our own fear of making the call. Hence, the real challenge is to do the self-management work necessary to "make" oneself make the call.

I recently came across a quote by William Burnham that sums up the issue here:

> The most drastic and usually the most effective remedy for fear is direct action.

Put another way, the trick in cold calling is to MAKE the call, to make yourself do this particular thing by repressing, inhibiting or ignoring all the negative thoughts that come up that try to stop you!

Incremental Exposure

The telemarketing job in Walnut Creek was an early introduction to severe call avoidance. I was filled with dread and severe chest pain just at the thought of making those calls. It took me a long time to overcome that feeling, but the one lesson I learned was that if you face a threat, (in this case an imaginary threat), gradually, with incrementally increased exposure, you learn to cope, especially as you learn that what you THINK is threatening really isn't. In reality, people are rarely rude, and you can handle rejection and failure. It passes, after all, to be replaced by the anticipated event of the next call. The more you call, the more self confidence grows; and the sales that occur as a result of calling are a more than adequate reward for the pain endured to acquire this skill.

The challenge here is learning how to endure the short-term discomfort of initiating contact with a prospect when you are vulnerable to negative evaluation and rejection. We need some sort of shield to protect ourselves and help achieve the objective of the call. One type of shield is your attitude towards calling and asking for the business. Some callers feel that calling puts them in a down power position, that calling is like a double edged sword where one is put in a position to have to cope with a possible "no" response, with no recourse if one gets that "no" answer except to keep answering objections and trying to "sell" the prospect. Both the initiation and the request make you vulnerable to the pain of rejection; it's as if you have deliberately put yourself in harm's way.

The irony is that to gain the advantage of a more effective voice, a more far reaching voice that is heard by your prospects, you need to first make the request that they lend you an ear, that they hear your proposition. For many salespeople, though, the fear of rejection, of the customer saying, "No, I don't want to buy," is probably the greatest fear of all. For most it means failure, wasted time, energy and effort. And somehow, while rejection is seen intellectually as just another refusal of an offer that is not currently needed, emotionally it is received as a slap in the face.

In the cold call, making the request for an appointment, even a request just to hear one's pitch, may itself be discomforting because it is often accompanied by shame and guilt. One salesperson I interviewed in the financial consulting field illustrated this point of view:

> I hate to initiate requests to prospects since I am so guilt ridden about the activity of requesting itself since it seems so intrusive. Which is to say I am ashamed of myself for doing this. I am not accepting of my own wishes to impose on people with financial advice. So, when I go make these requests… which I have guilt feelings about doing… and then I get rejected, it just

seems to confirm what I don't want to admit... the unacceptability of myself, of my own desires, interests, even of myself as a salesperson.

This case illustrates the shame many people have about calling and requesting, as if there were some stigma attached to doing this. In my view, this shame is the emotional truth of call avoidance for many callers. It is this shame that would have them believe that others might think of them as a mere peddler, a lesser human being who is dishonored by others who see calling as socially gauche, gawky or tactless.

An attitude of acceptance of oneself as a telesales representative or inside salesperson is the critical issue. It is your shield! In sales, you must learn to accept this role on the grounds that it is a legitimate business practice that has been around since the invention of the telephone. In short, it is OK! You cure yourself of the stigma by embracing the role fully. It doesn't hurt to realize as well that the sales function itself is crucial to the success of any capitalist society. Admirers of sales people say: "Nothing happens until something is sold!"

Do It Anyway!

It is false fears and imagined threats that people use as excuses, consciously or unconsciously, not to make a call. They are trapped by this false fear and don't know it. The reason they don't know it is because they haven't made enough calls to discover its falsity. Rather, the imagined disapproval is used as an excuse and rationalization not to make the calls. The only way you will be able to make the calls is to make the calls and find out for yourself that your fears are false!

4. Coping with Personal Doubt and Rejection

If you are like most people, the prospect of giving a public speech, introducing yourself to strangers, or making cold calls always seems full of overwhelming obstacles. In fact, it has taken me a long time and lots of personal experience to sort out all the possible barriers that must be overcome. I call them "villains"because in every instance they seem to operate to stop, sabotage or otherwise undermine your calling efforts. These villains hide in the back of your mind like a troll under a bridge. Almost always, these obstacles relate to our private fears of disapproval, rejection or outright failure.

However, I am pleased to report that it does get better with time. Obstacles usually melt away as one gains experience and perspective. Over the years, my old dread of making calls returns from time to time, even after thousands of calls. But I can say that the problem comes back so infrequently that now it's no longer an issue. But it's not always easy, it's not automatic and I'm still just a bit uncomfortable sometimes as I prepare to initiate a particularly important call to a high status prospect. But I find now that if I make a lot of calls in a short period of time the dread is hardly an issue. I'm too busy dialing and making calls to think about it! The lesson here is to make lots of calls quickly and cold calling will become easier for you that much sooner.

My next villain was dealing with objections, the "no" and the "not interested." Pushing forward beyond the "no" is still a challenge for me; for others, the "close" or asking for the order is a bigger challenge. I must say I like the approach supported by Bill Good, *Prospecting Your Way to Sales Success,* (Scribner, 1997) of just going after the red cherries (the low hanging fruit). Here you don't really have to do much persuasion or objection handling because you only deal with those who are or will soon be in the market. You do this by calling only qualified leads. But, as you evolve in sales skills and become a real pro, you will learn to effectively deal with objections. If you develop confidence in handling "no" and "not interested," you will be more likely to pick up the phone.

Another obstacle is the threat of rebuff and rejection because your offering is of no interest to the prospect. Unprotected by the claims of some prior relationship with a third party, tenuous though that may be, the cold approach sets one up for the maximum likelihood of failure. Making yourself vulnerable to a real or imaginary threat is a hard thing to do. And so the encounter with rejection triggers all sorts of negative feelings and thoughts of retreat. It's pretty easy to imagine the worst and feel even more timid as a result. My own encounters with rejection have activated my own self-doubts and wish to flee. Rejection appears to be worth avoiding. After all, it hurts; it feels bad, and makes one feel small, cowed and bitter. I remember door knocking mid-morning in a street in Oakland on a sunny day, realizing that I was all alone out there, enduring the rejection by myself while my peers had real jobs in downtown office parks and skyscrapers. In face to face prospecting, rejection is a personal encounter between yourself and your own insecurities. The psychologist Karen Horney argues convincingly that rejection is much harder to bear for those who are very insecure in the first place.

Whether the rude rejection happens on the phone or face to face, it's just as bad. I had a very deflating reaction when I called a restaurant once at noontime and interrupted the cooks during a horrendous argument. Needless to say, they got rid of my call in very short order. It's comforting to know the prospect is rejecting your proposition, not you personally. But sometimes it's hard to know that at an emotional level. And, of course, you don't know if the rejection is aimed at you or rather is tied to something going on in the environment into which you call.

It's not the rejection that's the problem, but how we react to it. At first, I found that all my reactions to rejection were negative. I felt defenseless and powerless to change the event. Over time, while I did get better at convincing a prospect to at least hear me out, the experience of rejection remained constant and unremitting. What changed was that I came to accept it as a cost of doing business this way. It went with the territory. I couldn't change the fact that I was being rejected, but I could change the way I felt about it by reframing the experience. I also learned that if I kept thinking this way, I would almost always find someone eventually that day who was friendly and would agree to an appointment.

Fear of Disapproval

In cold calling, it is difficult to predict how the other will respond. However, it is rare that the response is indeed a rude one. I suspect that the norms of politeness, especially in calling business to business, protect one from the likelihood of receiving an unmannerly reply. I myself have made thousands of cold calls and can count on the fingers of one hand the number of times I have been treated rudely. There are, of course, exceptions to this rule. Recently a commercial real estate agent told me she encounters lots of impatience calling on renters and building managers because other agents and brokers looking for business contact them so frequently. Generally, though, I find that in business-to-business calls, the reception is more civil because they rely on the telephone themselves and are open to business from 9:00 to 5:00, when "open" means ready to receive calls. Direct-to-consumer calls are a different story, especially when calling into residential areas between 6:00 and 7:30 in the evening. Here the likelihood of a firm rebuff or an impatient response is higher. In fact, I know some direct salesfolk who refuse to make these calls and only make business-to-business calls.

This fear of disapproval is made worse if one has a low opinion of one's own merits or lacks enough confidence in the value of a product or service to pick up the phone. I have met many newly minted salespeople who both are uncertain of themselves and lack basic product knowledge. They tend to shrink from contact with prospects because of lack of confidence and a suspicion that the identity of a salesperson is "less than" other professionals. This makes them ineffective or lacking in the presence with which to carry through the sales call process with confidence and aplomb. Typically, the giveaway is in tone of voice. It becomes meek and hesitant, as if some terrible threat is lurking close by and they become so preoccupied with questions of their own survival that putting up a good front is next to impossible.

The opposite tendency is to be presumptuous or unduly confident, taking something for granted or being forward or overconfident of one's own opinion or conduct. Sometimes one may go so far as to develop brazen assertiveness bordering on obnoxiousness. I find, for example, that in the financial services industry there seems to be a high percentage of overly aggressive callers who try to overwhelm their prospects with energy, expertise and chutzpa. On the other hand, I find that one of the unanticipated benefits of doing a great amount of cold calling is that I am much more at ease meeting and introducing myself to strangers at mixers, leads groups and Chambers of Commerce events. I am, in short, much more forward and outgoing with people face to face because I have encountered so many new people "voice to voice," without negative consequences and often with very positive results. I have become more thick-skinned. I sometimes feel that I am attracted to cold calling for its positive developmental potential. It is a valuable skill because of its impact on the rest of you. It builds character, at least of the sort that arms you for rejection and criticism. And as Shakespeare said, "No might nor greatness in mortality can censure scape."

Some callers regard cold calling as an improper invasion of privacy. Because of this, they believe they will be criticized, either openly or silently by the prospect who will be upset with their rudeness and not want to buy their service or product, or worse, hang up on them. The prospector becomes timid and anxious in the same way a shy person is daunted at the prospect of performing in front an audience, but for a different reason. Instead of personal inadequacy, he or she fears the accusation of breaking the rules of polite society.

In fact, I suspect that due to the modern annoyance at telephone solicitors and the play the media gives to mocking the telephone sales rep, cold callers often come to think of themselves as the social outlaws of the modern world. They may perceive themselves as breaking the rules of etiquette pertaining to the rules of entrance to private, social space. (I hasten to add this pertains mostly to consumer calls, not to business-to-business calls that have far more acceptability). Here's how some other people feel about it:

I hate the idea of calling cause I just know the prospect will be pissed off at me for interrupting their dinner or something; I won't call unless I have to, and even then only during 9:00 to 5:00. (Mortgage Broker)

It really makes me cringe to contemplate calling someone I don't know because I know I am made uncomfortable when someone cold calls me. I don't like presenting myself as a pushy salesperson only interested in making a buck and thereby interrupting the sanctity of a personal living space. (Financial Planner)

There is no telling how the prospect might respond when you break into their time, space or activity. You never know what they are up to. It makes me uncomfortable, especially with homeowners; I just feel it's always better if they know you will be calling first.(Insurance Agent)

Fear of Self-Disclosure

Many potential cold callers worry how they will answer a question or objection for which they have no scripted, pat answer. They fear revealing a lack of intellectual competence or selling skills. Whatever it is for each person, the initiation of a cold call evokes the risk of negative judgment of one's abilities. Thus, some are nervous about making the call due to a particular type of performance anxiety: a specific situational phobia that pertains, in this case, to picking up the phone to make a cold call. Some can make a cold approach to a stranger without difficulty when it's face to face; but by phone, voice to voice, they clam up!

This aversion can be especially acute when the proposition is a self-promotion where the callers sell their own services. Self-advertisement is quite different from the proposition presented by the telemarketers who call at night offering yet another credit card or solicitation for some non-profit enterprise. Some of my small business associates hire telemarketers who, without much training or preparation, can call on a list to set up appointments seemingly without much resistance or trouble. Yet the owner, when he or she tries to call, is tongue tied and finds any excuse not to call. What is the difference? When you have no personal investment in the product or service, and are being paid an hourly wage to find prospects, it's just a form of work; but when you are also the provider of the service, then there is far more ego investment. More is at risk because of the close association between your identity as the caller and the product or service that you are providing.

But in sales the salient question is whether the benefits you are offering are valid and whether the features will really produce the benefits you promise, whether delivery and implementation will happen as you say. In many instances there is no question.

In other cases, however, where the promised benefit is contingent upon the performance of the delivering party, the benefit may not always be reliably forthcoming. This especially applies to the management consultant, CPA or sales trainer where the question arises of competence, experience and the evidence in the eyes of others that the provider has delivered what was promised.

In the training field, for example, the efficacy of the benefit almost always depends on the willingness of the trainee to apply the lessons to his or her own work. In these cases, the position of the salesperson is precarious. Promises are made that may or may not be fulfilled. This can cause an element of doubt to creep into the conversation, breeding even more hesitancy and fear on the part of the caller. This in turn impacts the delivery of the sales message, which can negatively influence one's readiness to pick up the phone the next time. A vicious circle indeed, and a difficult obstacle to overcome.

The Obstacle of Self-Handicapping Beliefs

Frequently, prospectors who don't want to make cold calls excuse themselves from doing so by using the argument that it is somehow improper to call on strangers. They feel that if there is no apparent need established before the call to legitimize it, then it is perfectly excusable not to pick up the phone. It's really a form of "self-handicapping"and is one of the more common obstacles causing call avoidance. Self-handicapping is a term used in psychological literature to refer to the tendency to claim impediments prior to the performance of something (like public speaking, or dieting), in order to avoid doing those kinds of things. The obstacle here is the belief that the call will be unwelcome for whatever reason. As long as we assume this belief to be true, we won't make the call.

At the moment of picking up the phone there are sometimes thoughts that come up that may give us pause, like: "What if the prospect is busy? What if he or she doesn't want to talk to me now? This call will be a waste of time. They probably don't want to do business anyway. Everyone else is calling them. Rejection is very likely [and I'm not in the mood for any more rejection!]." These thoughts impede the calling activity, either slowing down the rate of calling or causing it to stop altogether.

Other forms of self-handicapping take place when callers: Don't want to make cold calls because they don't like receiving these types of calls at home in the evening; feel that calling as a form of follow up to direct mail is too labor intensive; say they don't have the time; think it isn't worthwhile to call because you can't get through voicemail.

What are the effects of self-handicapping in this manner? The result is usually failure to make any calls! Failure justified with a self-handicap protects self-esteem. It provides the excuse for a poor outcome, or for not trying to implement a cold calling strategy. If you lack adequate prospects, or sufficient income, could it be because you are self-handicapping yourself? Self-ascribed handicaps say that not making cold calls is due to factors over which we have no control. Calling makes us feel funny, or we can't speak because of some unconscious block, such as being unable to accept the salesperson identity for oneself.

Although all these maneuvers to not make calls can fool you into believing that it's OK not to call, the end result is likely to be a lot of guilt and self criticism for falling down on the job. Over the years I have struggled to short circuit these rationalizations. Initially, I found no escape from feeling that I should be able to do this activity. Somehow I never succumbed to the temptation of just quitting, which was often appealing!

There were times when I felt that I was caught in an endless, inescapable loop. I would resolve to call, find I couldn't, and then be punished by the tormenting consciousness of guilt and self-criticism. I saw myself as being weak and cowardly for not being willing to do this seemingly simple task. I would then analyze some possible reasons for being stuck, think I had it figured out, and make new resolves only to be faced with yet more resistance. I managed to break out of this loop by gradually dissolving my negative beliefs through acting to get feedback from the real world that proved their falseness. Goethe had it right, "Truth is action."

Facing the Fear of Futility

Another obstacle to cold calling can be the fear that one's efforts in making the call will never come to any positive conclusion. It can be easy to become discouraged and disheartened by too much calling that seems to have no yield. With a readiness to find any reason to stop, this apparent futility is a tempting option. One must remind oneself that the nature of the cold calling "beast" is that some ups and downs are inevitable. In my experience, some days will yield lots of contacts, and many interested prospects; other days will drag on with a seemingly endless series of rejections. This apparent loss of time or seeming waste of time can be difficult to justify.

50

Without a system of record keeping, a cold caller can be easily deceived into believing that cold calling never works and that the entire enterprise is useless. Cold calling tests the capacity to endure non-rewarding activity for a long period. Despite the fact that calling ultimately does work, the part of the mind that does not want to engage in the activity blinds one to phantom futility.

One becomes faced with his own disinclination which is based on a false perception derived from a too limited sample of operations. Perceiving a predominence of constant failures, one is led to the false conclusion that the activity is inevitably unproductive. This is not the case, but you have to prove it to yourself by making enough calls to demonstrate its falsity. Many people are unwilling to do this. The combination of fear of disapproval and a sense of futility keeps them from it.

Let's examine a real estate example. You are looking for people willing to list their property and you call every night starting at 5:00 p.m. and you ask the prospect: "Do you know anyone now or in the future who is interested in selling their property?" Night after night you call for an hour and seemingly get nowhere. Yet, for every 100 calls over time, you do get four leads, though they are all still in the future. But you want and are expecting a positive response right away, and so you become quickly disappointed and give up. Sound familiar?

The two problems here are unrealistic expectations and lack of record keeping. Cold calling is an investment that will pay off in the long term. The way you prove to yourself that it does work is to keep careful records of your calls. For most people, the problem is that they think they are held back by some mysterious force that prevents them from calling. And not understanding why, they don't know how to attack the problem. Because of our natural disinclination to make the calls, any reasons (even false ones) are eagerly grasped as a way to avoid having to make any calls at all.

Recognizing Unconscious Beliefs

Even after we overcome the aforementionned obstacles, there is sometimes a core, unconscious negative belief that can block calling activity. Mine was that the prospect, once she or he found out what I wanted, would be furious and scornful and that I wouldn't be able to handle it. In therapeutic terms this is an instance of transference where one is allowing an old attitude developed in childhood to influence adult communications. Only after many, many calls did I manage to prove to myself that this wouldn't happen. As a result of this feedback, the overall sense of inferiority and lack of self-confidence was gradually lifted. The norms of politeness do protect you; but you don't know this for sure until you have tested the waters by making lots of calls.

Overcoming Your Resistance to Making Calls

The feeling of dread and apprehension before a calling period is like no other. Unlike a toothache, which can be unremitting and only gradually lessen, this feeling of dull dread can be instantly corrected by just simply not making any cold calls. The pain of calling can be instantly stopped, yet to stop is to undermine one's pursuit of new prospects. Calling can sometimes evoke a battleground mentality where one experiences at least two parts of the self in conflict… one wanting to flee to reduce the pain, the other wanting to stick it out, to persist in the face of fear and doubt. What one hopes is that by forcing oneself to endure this feeling a little while longer, something new and exciting will come along, particularly a promising lead or prospect that by itself will put to an end this feeling of dread. All of us who have experienced prolonged bouts of calling have had the happy event occur just before giving up for the day when we have suddenly uncovered a pleasant prospect who welcomes our proposition.

But forcing oneself to stay at it is itself sometimes an enormous struggle which is difficult to manage because of "approach-avoidance conflict", the feeling of wanting and not wanting simultaneously. I have at times in the past felt totally immobilized by this feeling, yet could not flee because no rationalization was available that would permit such an action. One feels caught between the devil and the deep blue sea.

Protecting Your Ego Yet Wanting More Prospects

The resistance to calling may persist and be maintained by an underlying conflict between the desire to make the call and various fears of what might happen if the call is made. Until that conflict is resolved, the resistance continues. Resistance, which for cold callers mostly takes the form of procrastination and avoidance, means that some kind of danger is impending or is thought to be immanent; the resistance is to protect the person against the humiliation of failure or disapproval, or some other psychic risk. For the prospector, resistance may be an expression of the fear of failure, or the fear of giving unintended offense. The resistance, or avoidance, is an acting out of the conflict between honoring the wish to accelerate the production of new leads and these fears. But caving in to the resistance evolves into self-attacks and guilt for the seeming cowardice of not making the calls. The resistance may be said to be a symbolic response to an unconscious conflict between the desire to make the call and fear of the prospect's rage, ridicule and scorn. And it functions to protect the person from the recognition of certain unbearable ideas, most especially the notion that one is some kind of coward for not making the calls.

Unfortunately, the avoidance only delays the renunciation of the inappropriate fantasy that business can be expanded without finding new prospects to whom one has not yet been introduced. In business, the fond but usually inappropriate hope is that you will be able to sustain your business by word of mouth prospects alone. The avoidance sustains the continuing search for referral leads or other sources of prospects that cannot be as readily found at such a low cost.

Fear, Guilt and Self-Criticism

The worst feature of all this conflict is that it produces a roller coaster ride of fear, guilt and self-criticism. Fear, because of what might be encountered in the calling activity, followed by guilt and self-criticism for escaping the activity when it becomes too burdensome. The great thing about overcoming cold call avoidance is that these feelings go away as one begins to make progress in finding new prospects and new business.

I know that in listing all the obstacles to calling, I may have created an impression of overall helplessness and powerlessness that the reader may find difficult to overcome and depressing to contemplate. Yet there is hope based on the abilities you all have to:

- Make a meaningful presentation of the features and benefits of your proposal to the prospect.
- Assert yourself as a sales person who has something valuable to offer that may meet the needs of the prospect.
- Feel that you deserve to succeed.
- Create mechanisms to nurture and comfort yourself in the face of negative experiences associated with cold calling.

Above all, be reassured that millions of salespeople have gone before you who have eventually overcome, at least periodically, the internal demons that can deter initiating calls and implemented a consistent program of cold calling. What becomes of the capacity to generate new initiatives to contact business prospects in the face of so much self-discounting?

Once when I was door knocking in a suburb of Oakland, the man swung open the door and told me he wasn't interested in buying anything I had to offer, regardless of what it was, and said "good bye" and slammed the door. Ouch! I recall slinking back to my car and going straight home, intensely humiliated. I recently met a woman who said she burst into tears when someone was rude to her on the phone. It hurts. But it passes. Yet these experiences leave a residue of pain that lodge somewhere in the unconscious ready to send out warning signals just as you contemplate making the next call. There are now, fortunately, proven tactics that will enable you to handle these aversive memory traces so that you can be liberated enough to make the call. You will learn about them as you read on in this book.

5. Overcoming Call Avoidance
Self-Regulation and the
GIRDA Formula for Action

After all my incarnations as an advance man, or an approach
specialist, if you will, in real estate, the seminar business, home
improvement sales and consulting work, I had accumulated
quite a lot of experience battling my fears and doubts around
cold calling. I wouldn't say I had overcome every obstacle, but I
had achieved sufficient understanding to at least have suitable
labels for all of my inner opponents. Next came the challenge to
control them, or at least to believe that it was possible to
manage them enough so I could make consistent steps forward.

Through a painstaking process of trial and error... from which I
hope to spare you... I devised the GIRDA formula for
successful cold calling. "G" stands for Goal and designates the
need to set daily goals. "I" stands for Incrementally increasing
your goals. "R" stands for Record-keeping that documents your
effort. "D" stands for Distancing yourself from the "inner critic"
who doesn't want you to make the calls. "A" stands for
Accountability, partnering with a mentor, coach, coworker or
friend. The formula will be elaborated as I discuss
implementing specific strategies and tactics.

So much of the task of facing adversity is making up for the lost time you spend inventing rationalizations for your stagnation. I don't know where this idea of self-regulation or self-management came from, but over the years it has definitely helped me. Perhaps my experience and efforts to successfully control my long term tobacco addiction was the process that suggested that self-managing an inner conflict was a key to success. Conflict between warring tendencies is always there, in smoking cessation as well as overcoming call avoidance. The issue is what are you going to do to seize control and not let your tendencies control you.

Managing call avoidance is first a matter of understanding its causes. We have gone over a good many of these and have found that the causes are mainly related to our own inner fears and beliefs that function to impede the calls. Recently, I had a conversation with an outside sales rep at a client's office. He was assigned to give me 20 companies to call cold in order to uncover new business. He let me know that he believed that these calls were a waste of time; hence he didn't make them himself. Since he believed that cold calling is ineffective, he made no calls. No calls of this sort mean't fewer leads and less revenue.

Beliefs like these just further enable a caller's paralysis. How do I know this? Because I used to have the same belief! But by forcing myself to make lots of calls, I eventually discovered it wasn't true. Cold calling is effective; it's just a question of doing enough over the long haul.

The specific form of these fears and beliefs differs for each person. The challenge is to find ways to regulate them so that rather than remaining automatic, there is a shift towards control and moving forward. I believe that fear of disapproval, fear of rejection, fear of authority, fear of giving offense, fear of unwelcome intrusion, etc., are all target fears that must be regulated. Along with these fears, the belief that calling is futile and ineffective must be controlled as well.

Behavioral Control

One of the best answers I have found to the challenge of control is in the literature on the psychology of self-management and self-regulation. B.F. Skinner argued long ago that an individual can be said to successfully control his behavior when he can effectively influence the variables of which the behavior is a function. In the case of cold calling, the variables that chiefly determine call avoidance are again the inner fears and negative beliefs of the caller. For Skinner, the controlling process involves arranging environmental conditions to increase the possibility of receiving positive reinforcement. In the case of cold calling, the key is to arrange the environment of the call so that the prospector *thinks* the call will be accepted. In this way you fool your belief system into permitting you to make the call. But how can you do this?

One way to warm up the call so that it is easier to make is to let the callee know that you will be calling. By telegraphing that a call is coming, you can convince yourself that the call will be more readily accepted. In some cases, the call is expected if your letter or marketing piece got the attention and interest of the prospect. A variation on this approach is simply to send by mail or e-mail some information with a note stating that you *will call* as a follow up. This is a great way to knock down one of the obstacles to calling… that the call is not expected. This is especially helpful when calling on corporate clients. The data from my own experience and that of my clients suggests your success rate is likely to be better when calling as a follow up to an introductory letter or e-mail than when calling cold.

I recommend this approach to neophyte cold callers. It is true that the prospect may not have read the material or may not recall even seeing the piece. But you don't know that when you make the call. It's easy to condition yourself to believe that she will be expecting your call. This can make all the difference in your willingness to pick up the phone.

Self-Regulation of Your "Inner States"

Psychologist Albert Bandura asserts that people pursuing learning goals typically set certain standards of behavior for themselves and self-administer rewarding or punishing consequences depending on whether their performance falls short, matches, or exceeds self- prescribed demands. In Bandura's approach, self-monitoring and self-reinforcement are essential to the self-control process.

Self-regulation or self-control may be defined as exercising some restraint or direction over one's actions, emotions or thoughts. It often implies conflict, where one must *will* oneself away from one's dominant inclination. For example, stopping smoking or reducing alcohol and drug dependency. In these cases, one is regulating the contrary impulses of temptation and desire. For cold callers, it's just the opposite regulatory issue... it's about "forcing" yourself to do something another part of you detests.

In the case of cold calling, this self-management is best facilitated by having certain things in place before you start a calling session. You need uninterrupted time, a good script, and a list of names and phone numbers in front of you. In my earlier experiences as a rookie caller, I found it difficult to go back and forth between calling and non-calling activities. The excuses not to make the call would come raging forward whenever I stopped to do something else and then tried to get back on track. Paralysis would set in again and I would find and use any excuse not to resume the calling. It was only when I figuratively "chained myself" to the desk and focused only on the calling that I was able to move forward. Blocking out dedicated calling times will definitely help you make more calls. It certainly has helped me.

Another useful definition of self-management is that it is a process by which the individual deliberately employs certain cognitive or behavioral tactics to reach a goal that would otherwise be difficult to attain. This is because of social forces or our own habits that impede or discourage its pursuit. I like this approach because it is at the level of behavior and thought that self-regulation is best achieved. In order for these techniques to work, they must be firmly based on an understanding of why so many people are so loath to make the cold calls that will increase their income.

My Theory of Call Avoidance

My theory of call avoidance is as follows. There is a conflict between your wish to make the call and your fears of doing so. The way that many people resolve this conflict is to procrastinate, which does take away the threat, but fails to get the prospector more leads or sales. The challenge is the find a better resolution that somehow deals with the anxiety and garners more prospects.

This conflict is often concealed by the fact that the prospector is held captive by a variety of erroneous ideas concerning the possible consequences of cold calling, but doesn't know it. He is blind to his own captivity and victimization. Because of inability to perceive the conflict, the caller does not know what is holding him back; he experiences only the feelings of avoidance or aversion and feels blocked by some "mysterious force" that prevents him from calling. By understanding that this conflict exists, the way is opened to explore different ways to move ahead. I know this is easy to say but hard to do. The challenge is to find a resolution that deals with the anxiety but permits pursuit of the dreaded activity at the same time.

When I first went door knocking in the suburbs of Oakland looking for prospects for real estate, I would start at about 4:00 in the afternoon, just as people were coming home from work. To settle my nerves, I used to stop in a bar and have a couple of beers before starting my campaign. Unfortunately, as time went on I found myself spending more time in the bars and less time canvassing. This was not a functional or healthy way of dealing with my nerves.

Until they found a way around it, many of my friends found other less dysfunctional ways to procrastinate. Mary Lou Evans, an insurance agent for State Farm, used to find that it was very easy for her to defer her calls and instead bone up on her product knowledge by reading journals and newsletters pertinent to her industry. Brian O'Brien with Cellular One used to find himself giving in to the impulse to write proposals for prospective clients rather than picking up the phone. Jack Brodsky, a real estate agent, reviewed the MLS catalogue to make sure he knew of all new listings that might be of interest to his buyers... but he did that instead of cold prospecting. We all have our preferred ways of procrastinating.

If Procrastination Is Not the Answer, Then What Is?

When most of us face something threatening we don't want to do, we procrastinate or find a substitute activity. One of my friends in the securities field, Joe Murray, claimed he was the most creative procrastinator he knew. He would go to the bank, talk on the phone, write letters, and make "to do" lists… anything to avoid picking up the phone to make cold calls. Those who have studied the matter say that procrastinators avoid taking action that is revealing of their abilities, skills or intellectual competence. In other words, they "hide out" to avoid being judged. Many procrastinating cold callers will resonate with this thought. As William James said: "With no attempt, there can be no failure; with no failure, there's no humiliation." Since many feel their sense of self-worth is related to their abilities, they avoid performances which might provoke a negative judgment and that would make them feel bad about themselves and their abilities. To perform at all risks negative evaluation, and hence it is thought more prudent to not take the risk, even though there may be negative consequences.

But this can be overcome by understanding this key point. ***The fear of negative evaluation, or other fears, are mostly false fears that can be disproved only by a program of gradually increased calling on cold prospects***. The best way to overcome call avoidance is by gradually building up your confidence to the point where you begin to understand that the negative thoughts that impede you from calling are actually false! But you won't ever know this secret for sure until you have the experience of making the calls.

Progressive Desensitization

The first solution to call avoidance is a behavioral solution and rests on the principle of ***progressive desensitization***. It involves making oneself less sensitive to rejection, failure and anticipated embarrassment. The first step is to establish a daily goal of how many calls you will make for the day. This number should be derived from your existing base calling rate, whether this is one or two calls per week, or 10 calls a day. Daily goal setting has been shown to be more effective than weekly or monthly intervals because daily goals, when achieved, are more immediately reinforcing than more distantly set goals.

I was not a big believer in goal setting until I found that it helps keep me focused and accountable. Goal setting will give you something to aim for and a method of measuring your progress, or lack thereof. Honesty compels me to admit that I wasn't always successful in reaching my goals. I started to do better when I came to agree with people who argue that all change is a matter of both progression and regression. Some days you do great, others you get into lulls and tributaries. Once I came to regard this as natural and expected, I wasn't as hard on myself when I fell short.

It is important to set an achievable call goal, and that the goal relates only to dials, not contacts, since dials can be controlled, while number of contacts with decision makers cannot.

The second step is to keep a record of the calls. Have a system for recording number of dials, and the fate of each call, whether you get through to the decision-maker, the result of the conversation, and callbacks. A calling sheet is reproduced here that I use and like. It constitutes a "behavioral doing" that gives you a sense of producing forward progress and positive results instead of endless rejection and discouragement.

A record system does several things. It helps you when the inevitable lulls hit and you begin to think that cold calling is a waste of time. It proves that your calls will produce more than just voice mail and callbacks. With a record of your calls over the weeks and months you can see that calling is like a roller coaster ride, sometimes up and sometimes down, but pretty predictable in the long run. What appears to be evidence of futility turns into an understandable lull when records are kept. Otherwise you are likely to give up too soon and too easily.

A record keeping system or call sheet also permits you to figure your success ratios so you can determine how many calls it takes to get a sale, how many to book an appointment, and so on. This information allows you to calculate the dollar value of each dial. I once worked with a real estate agent who hadn't made any cold calls in 17 years in the business, but finally decided it was time. Her records showed she made 680 dials, got 29 leads and two listings. When the properties sold, her commission was $6,000 dollars… that worked out to be about $10 for every time she picked up the phone!

The concept of making $10 for every dial constitutes a far more empowering meaning than to see it as just another opportunity to get to "no."Ironically, she became so busy with the results of her calling campaign that she gave up dialing. Unfortunately, cold calling tends to be the first thing that goes when times improve. A consistent program of cold calling, even at a low weekly activity level, will help protect against that feast or famine cycle that salespeople hate.

Probably the best reason for keeping records of your calls is to re-educate yourself, turning your fears into positive self-confidence. I've sat with clients and looked back at their record of hundreds, if not thousands of cold calls made over time, with no evidence that anything bad ever happened to them. In fact, what we did see was a steady progression of improved skill in cold calling, getting new business that way and seeing that it is a viable marketing strategy worthy of serious commitment.

You will find that keeping records and seeing improvement can become a source of pride and positive reinforcement for your calling activity. Bandura showed that self-motivation depends on daily goal setting and self-evaluative reactions-- pride or shame-- towards one's own behavior. Record keeping facilitates this process. In fact, for that self-evaluative reaction to take place you *need* standards against which to evaluate progress. Comparing your goals to your records constitutes such a standard and is the only practical way that positive (or negative) feelings can be achieved. Either outcome can be motivating. If you attain your goal, the positive feeling of self-pride becomes something you want to reproduce. If you fall short, the associated guilt acts as a goad to do better next time.

There are as many types of methods for recording your calls. The actual format isn't the most important thing; the key is in actually keeping the records. The following form is one I favor:

Daily Call Sheet

Date_____
Start Time _____
End Time _____

DIALS
1 2 3 4 5 6 7 8 9 10 11 12 13 14 15 16 17 18 19 20
21 22 23 24 25 26 27 28 29 30 31 32 33 34 35 36 37 38 39 40
41 42 43 44 45 46 47 48 49 50 51 52 53 54 55 56 57 58 59 60
61 62 63 64 65 66 67 68 69 70 71 72 73 74 75 76 77 78 79 80
81 82 83 84 85 86 87 88 89 90 91 92 93 94 95 96 97 98 99 100

COLD CONTACTS
1 2 3 4 5 6 7 8 9 10 11 12 13 14 15 16 17 18 19 20

CALL BACK CONTACTS: 1 2 3 4 5 6 7 8 9 10 11 12 13 14 15 16

REFERRAL CALL BACKS: 1 2 3 4 5 6 7 8 9 10 11 12 13 14 15 16

PROSPECTS
1 2 3 4 5 6 7 8 9 10 11 12 13 14 15 16 17 18 19 20

INFORMATION REQUESTS
APPOINTMENTS

1 2 3 4 5 6 7 8   1 2 3 4 5
9 10 11 12 13 14 15 16

PROSPECT CALL BACKS   REFERRAL
CALLS

1 2 3 4 5 6 7 8   1 2 3 4 5
9 10 11 12 13 14 15 16   6 7 8 9 10 11
17 18 19 20 21 22 23 24
25 26 27 28 29 30 31 32

More on Record Keeping

Recent studies have shown the crucial importance of record keeping for long-term behavior change. A study was done of the single factor most predictive of long-term behavior change and it was self-monitoring on a daily basis. (D.S. Kirschenbaum, "*Self Regulatory Failure*," in D.S. T. Baker and D.S. Cannon, eds., *Assessment and Treatment of Addictive Disorders*, Praeger, 1988).

Records function to keep you focused and give you a way of tracking the ups and downs of calling so that you do not become discouraged with the inevitable lulls and downturns when positive results seem hard to achieve. When you hit that inevitable lull, you know that it won't last and hopefully you avoid the feeling of discouragement and futility. My rule of thumb on lead generation is that if I don't get a couple of leads after an hour of calling, I either change my script to that target market, or I change the market.

But record-keeping alone isn't enough, at least judging by results reported in the social science journals. Self-regulatory failure is more the rule. In other words, people usually don't change in the absence of external constraint or accountability. They try to change on their own, do so for a short period of time, and then backslide or relapse. This is the case whether the target behavior is smoking cessation, weight loss, ending drug and alcohol abuse, or school study behavior. Or, for that matter, trying to overcome call avoidance!

This is definitely the pattern in cold call prospecting calls. Salespeople do it for a time, but as soon as the flow of business picks up, making calls is the first thing they abandon. Since the issue is initiation and not compliance with a system of authority, the risk is always there. So with no one watching other than his or her own conscience, the prospector begins to flag in his efforts. Unless committed to a goal of success, a valued principle or singular purpose that burns in his heart, the chances are great that the cold calling effort will decrease over time.

Sales managers seek to deal with this problem by some system of incentives, but this has the weakness of always needing to be renewed with some new competition, gimmick or the proverbial trip to Hawaii. "Self-motivation" is held up as the answer, but it is not easily achieved since compliance with one's own intentions is always a problem. One's own inner conflicts, doubts and fears always seem to undermine motivation. Hard work and discipline may be weakened by discouragement and a sense of futility, which always lurk in the wings with calling campaigns.

As I have said, a key component in the behavioral solution to managing call avoidance is incrementally increasing the calling rate. The standard or goal must be increased **gradually** to keep it as a motivator and to ensure that the anxiety level is not overwhelming. At the same time you find you can cope with the negatives long enough to disprove the false beliefs that kept you hostage to your fears. You find out, for example, that the possible rudeness you anticipated does not occur, or if it does you can handle it. Rejection, it turns out, *is bearable* and is simply the price you pay for getting to "yes".

I once made 15,000 cold calls over a two-year period. I had periods of discouragement and periods of exhilarating progress. The rejection, while unpleasant at times, was in the end, monetarily rewarding. I can say that because I kept records on all of those calls. When prospectors acquire an internal control orientation that leads them to set goals incrementally and develop a commitment to the process of calling every day, and recording those calls, they develop a sense of personal self-esteem. This is a feeling that they have control over what happens to them. Self-esteem in turn influences your willingness to make the next call. When perceived self-esteem is high, performance is better and there is less anxiety. The most desirable outcome is to get to the point where you prove to yourself that if you make the calls, good things will happen. Record keeping will help you accomplish that goal.

A Cognitive Solution to Call Avoidance

Of all the difficulties besetting the prospector looking for new contacts, none is more troublesome than those negative thoughts that float up whenever one reaches for the phone. This self-talk that we undergo, those rambling musings over what we did, didn't do, what we have to do, who we want to call, and so on, represents unvoiced speech directed at oneself. There are always two voices: the *inner critic* generating all the negative thoughts and beliefs that tend to stop us from calling; and, the *executive self,* the sub personality that produces all the justifications for making the calls.

It has been said elsewhere that we often bet our lives on the stories we tell ourselves about the world, but *rarely hear them* while they are being told. The inner dialogue that results from the idea of making cold calls goes something like:

- I don't want to make this call because I expect the prospect won't be available.
- He probably doesn't want to talk to me anyway; its probably not a good time to call.
- I bet she has already received lots of calls on this topic.
- I haven't had my second cup of coffee and they probably are all in a meeting now.
- I should send a letter instead and hope they will respond.
- This category of prospect has never brought my service in the past so they probably will say no anyway. But, I ought to make this call. I've run out of referral leads.
- I need new contacts to build my business and meet my financial goals for the year.

And so it goes. By all reports from those whom I have asked to monitor their inner self-talk during calling, the inner critic producing the negative thoughts is far stronger than the executive self that knows that this is a viable method of business development. The inner critic developed out of your childhood to protect you from various threats to life and limb whether these were parents, busy intersections, or school bullies. But now as an adult, your inner critic tends to hold you back. It inhibits, criticizes, weakens and generally discourages you from taking any initiative like cold calling. It constricts your ability to be creative. It stops you from taking risks because it makes you fear failure. It views your life as a series of mistakes waiting to happen. It undermines your courage to change and compares you unfavorably with others and makes you feel "less than."

As we constantly talk to ourselves about our prospecting, describing what is happening, what is going to happen, what should happen and what might happen, we tend to give in to all the warnings, excuses and rationalizations for why reaching for that phone is a bad idea. Calling is stopped because the story we tell ourselves about what will happen if we call is such a disheartening tale of futility and danger. Yet it is exactly this story that largely shapes how we feel and act about calling. Certainly the feelings we get from listening to these thoughts are those of doubt, fear and uncertainty. We become intimidated by this voice. Our own inner dialogue stops us in our tracks! By realizing that our story of what is going to happen controls our action, we can choose to change some of the negative elements, or at least test them out to see if the story line is true or false. It may be that the internal narrative is completely fictitious! By examining your self-talk, you can begin to question the underlying irrational beliefs that shape your responses and mood. And by reframing how you think about events, you can shift into a more positive mood.

The first step is to become more aware of your self-talk that is activated by calling prospects. One way to do this is by writing down a dialogue between your executive-self and your inner critic, a dialogue that focuses on the executive-self trying to persuade the inner critic of the advantages of making the call and the inner critic trying to set up roadblocks.

Such a dialogue might go like this:

> Executive Self (ES): Well, it's 10:00 am, a good time to start calling, so lets call this broker, how about it?
>
> Inner Critic (IC): No I don't think I'm quite ready yet. Let's write this letter instead, or how about another cup of coffee?
>
> ES: No, you're just procrastinating; come on, let's make this call. I know we need new prospects since business is starting to fall off.
>
> IC: Yah, but what about direct mail or going to leads groups. You don't really know that cold calling works, and besides we have enough referral leads already.
>
> EC: But that's just it; we don't have enough referral leads, we always run out, and anyway this prospect list

78

has already produced some good leads, so let's get started.

IC: I have to print out the call sheet; I'm not ready yet.

EC: Come on, you are just coming up with more and more flimsy excuses; this is ridiculous, you can do it, but you are giving in to an attitude that says this won't work.

IC: Damn right I am, because I know I don't like the feeling this activity produces in my gut… it makes me feel queasy; besides, it's so unprofessional to call… it's much better to write a marketing piece and send it by mail or e-mail… it's less intrusive.

EC: Nonsense, everyone knows that direct mail is only effective one half of one percent of the time, whereas telemarketing is six to eight percent effective. So let's call.

IC No, wait...

The challenge here is to regulate the statements of the inner critic that appear to have the strong weight of reason behind them, but are just transparent rationalizations. To rationalize is to invent a rational explanation for irrational behavior. The inner critic is expert at creating good reasons for not making the calls. But what you must realize is that *you have a choice* as to whether or not you comply with these rationalizations. ***You are not your inner critc!***

Silencing Your Inner Critic

One approach designed to silence your inner critic is to disidentify with and discount the negative thoughts it brings up. Why identify with it's musing as if you must indulge its every whim and point of view? You have a choice as to how you respond.

To disidentify from a thought process of which you are barely aware is not easy. I find that by assuming it will always be there (as it is for me even after having made thousands of calls), and understanding that it is just trying to protect me from imaginary threats to my security and self-esteem, I am more readily able to let these rationalizations go. You could think of some disidentification metaphors that convey disappearance, like pressing the delete button on a computer, or erasing a tape on a VCR, but the best solution is simply to take the action of going on to the next call.

To be able to discount these excuses and rationalizations means to know that at some level they are illegitimate, false and will only serve to sabotage your best interests! Why not take the attitude that sees these mental impediments as the ravings of scared child, an undeveloped part of the self that still views others as a threat, a danger to one's sense of integrity and worthiness?

You can also regulate this voice after you have become aware of its existence and have become convinced that it is standing in your way and protecting you from imaginary fears. You can do this by using a psychological technique called "thought stopping." In behavior therapy, this is a technique in which the therapist stops undesirable thought sequences by shouting, "STOP." The patient is then instructed to apply the technique to himself. (One variation on this approach is to wear a rubber band around your wrist and snap it vigorously every time one of these excuses comes up. A bit extreme perhaps, but you get the point).

Finally, finding replacement thoughts for those thoughts that you are busy trying to ignore is a positive step to take. You need to find substitute thoughts that are compelling and embody more positive emotions like hope and anticipation. Eighty percent of sales only happen after the twelfth contact. Let go of your fears and see what happens. If you know what your calling ratios are, then you know that it takes, on average, for instance, nine No's to make a sale. Then calling is just a process of piling through the No's! If you don't keep trying you will be letting yourself be run by others. Remember, he who dares, wins!

Your inner critic is a powerful voice that will always be there at some level. If you can manage to avoid arousing it in the first place, you are better off. Some callers hide the industry or job title of the prospect because of the associated meanings they've stored up with regard to those types of prospect that tend to stimulate negative scripts. For example, some callers are intimidated by high status prospects like CEO's or other "C" level officers. By hiding the affiliation of the callee, they circumvent this problem and can more efficiently move down their lists of prospects.

It also may be useful in managing your inner critic to get in touch with any other specific feelings you have in terms of calling, especially feelings of anger. For while you have every right to be furious with this archaic part of yourself that keeps you in servitude to your doubts and fears, you must step over these feelings to overcome your inner critic. You may need more than an ounce of bravado to do this, but it can be very empowering to "let go and see what happens." I would venture to say that everything that gets in the way of cold calling is a product of the inner critic: the doubts, reservations, fears, sense of futility, the weakness and sense of powerlessness. If you allow negative thoughts and judgments to run on, they make you weak and make you dependent on referral leads. How much better to be the autonomous producer of your own leads, always able to find new prospects by the simple device of merely picking up the phone!

Partnering for Accountability

Accountability is the final piece in our GIRDA formula for overcoming call avoidance. This can be difficult, especially for the entrepreneur or salesperson who needs to rely on his own volition and initiative to make these calls and is not subject to an employer's quota system which mandates a specific number of cold calls.

Goal setting, record keeping and dealing with the inner critic constitute the kind of regimen that one would be well advised to follow. Many of us meet any admonition to follow a specific procedure with rebellion, resistance or holding back. This may be due to fear of failure, or even fear of success. It may be a defense against threats to self-esteem that might be encountered if one tries and has few or no results. For some there is a need for a comfortable routine and doing something new threatens that sense of normality. For others there is the matter of lack of faith in the prescription, the feeling that somehow the method or treatment might work for others, but not for them, because they are "different." There is a need for a mechanism that sustains effort and rewards compliance. And the best mechanism I have discovered is accountability.

Accountability means having someone you can talk to about your calling activity, someone you can set goals with and report back to. I like to call this relationship a training partnership. It can be put in place with a friend, work associate, business coach or mentor. I often do it for clients. It is best to have a written contract in which you promise another person to achieve a certain goal each week. The contract should be renewable at your discretion to avoid dependency.

You'll want to be able to reach a sustainable level of activity, but it may take a month or two before this is attainable on your own. To have the support and guidance of a coach until this autonomy is reached is empowering and avoids the fantasy that you can do this work on your own. I have found it works best to agree in advance on the number of calls to be made, by when, and the specific times at which you will be in contact with your accountability partner. Then sign this contract, date it and both of you keep a copy.

6. Using Scripts and Adjusting Your Attitude

When I first started working on the problem, I didn't believe that a script had much to do with managing call avoidance. After I presented my first public seminar a broker came up and said "But what about scripts?" I told him I didn't think they were that important. I was wrong.

Since then, I have come to believe that I need some sort of bridge to get through the first 15 second, the most awkward moments in any cold call. A good script serves this function in that it gets the ball rolling. I used to "wing it," but found that being tongue-tied didn't help advance my cause. I believe it is necessary to have an effective script that is a natural self-expression and yet doesn't turn off your inclination to call. Even after many calls, the importance of a good script remains. You may change it from time to time based on results, but you always need a strong opening line.

The script helps in overcoming call avoidance because it gives you an avenue of approach that opens the way for further questions and relationship building later in the call. Part of the feeling of security that you desparately need in the beginning stages of the call comes from the conviction that you know what you are going to say, and that your line of talk has a good chance of being effective in attaining the objective of the call. In business to business calls, which constitute 80 percent of all telemarketing calls, the idea is to be business like, get to the point quickly and uncover the possible need of the prospect.

Your script is a vehicle for getting you where you want to go. It helps open a conversation, states your intent and immediately establishes credibility with the prospect. If you have a very young-sounding voice, or you represent a company no one has ever heard of, then boosting credibility is extremely important. Some people see a script as like a crutch, but a necessary one, especially early in your calling career.

Over the years, I have developed many scripts for myself and for clients. A good script helps produce a comfort level that is critical in helping you make the call. You've got to know what you are going to say. An interesting side effect of database management programs like ACT or Goldmine is that some callers feel they are slowed down by the necessity to document their calls. But, such a database program can help you personalize your script by including a reference to the history of your interaction with this prospect. So once you get the ball rolling, databases can help eliminate your reliance on totally "canned" scripts. The bottom line here is that the most effective callers still use a script that they have fine tuned over time and vary just a bit for each prospect.

For this next section I am much indebted to William Good, author of *Prospecting Your Way to Sales Success,* Scribners and Sons, 1986. Mr. Good has sold everything from securities to real estate investments by phone. His breadth of knowledge and sales success inspires confidence in his method. It is one I use myself and highly recommend. (I will not go on at length about his approach here but leave the reader to go to his book for the most thorough presentation).

The Essential Components of a Good Script

A good script is extremely important to your calling success because of its impact on call effectiveness. How effective you are in turn impacts how willing you are to pick up the phone. Effectiveness and calling rates are the two main determinants of sales revenue. In my own calling career, I often came to doubt the effectiveness of my script, or felt that I didn't "sound like me." The question of effectiveness was always in the back of my mind and I would try all sorts of little changes to fine-tune the script to optimize my chances for success. After reading Good's book and following his approach, I have become convinced that he has captured the essential components of an effective script.

The best way to define a good script is that it is a pre-planned and well-practiced dialogue that arouses the listener's interest and permits you to bridge the gap between 'hello' and the initial question. In Good's view, the universe is made up of three types of prospects: those who are immediately interested in your solution (the "red cherries"); those who lack the money or decision making power, but are interested ("green cherries"); and the "pits" (those who express no interest and need to be re-contacted in 60 to 90 days).

This way of dividing up the prospect world is not very exacting, but it does bear on the question of who to concentrate on in your calls and on the more important question of how to qualify your prospects. As a cold caller for many different companies and offers, I have found that it is always helpful to know whether the person you are talking to has the power or the money to make decisions. For example, I have had a lot of experience dealing with trade show leads and business conference leads of all sorts. Many attendees who come by a booth and leave their contact particulars may or may not be in the decision-making loop but they may be the only contacts you have. At least you have their name and company affiliation and you know by their attendance at the show that they may have an interest in your proposition.

You need to quickly determine whether they are the decision-maker or not. If not, you can find out if they will lead you to someone who is.

One objective of the script, then, is to achieve a contact with the prospect that at least leads to some interest as indicated by a willingness to receive information, and at the most, leads to an appointment. According to Good, a great script designed to do just that contains four parts.

The first part is the introduction in which you state your name and the company you are with and give a one-sentence statement of who you are and what you do. For example. "My name is Joe Murray with XYZ company and we specialize in providing low cost advertising coupons"; or … "we specialize in providing alternative funding based on accounts receivables"; or… "we specialize in reducing stress in the workplace by providing custom designed, ergonomic furniture," etc.

The second part is the offer or hook of a special offer. This answers the implicit prospect question: "What's in it for me?" It is meant to provide the prospect a reason to stay on the phone. It is useful to understand that the prospect is looking for ways to get you off the phone and will jump you with a statement of rejection unless you can stay on long enough to tweak his or her interest. Some hooks could be a one-hour free consultation, a special, time limited discount offer, a reduced premium for a short period of time, or a free, no obligation trial offer. Some newly minted entrepreneurs or callers who are touchy about appearing too sales oriented may take offense at the notion of a hook. But it is a time-tested approach that works often enough to warrant its use. It offers a "foot in the door," especially if it can be tied to a benefit that the prospect needs at that moment. The *Encyclopedia Britannica* used to be famous for offering free books as a door opener, a way to get the attention of a prospect. Similarly, a hook or special offer serves the same purpose. Remember, you are only going after prospects who are immediately interested in your proposition, not those who keep putting you off with endless objections and false reassurances of interest. Of course there are occasions when a hook may not be appropriate because you have already determined from a lead form filled out at a trade show where the prospect's interests lie. Then it's just a matter of making the call to clarify that interest and set up the next step. You want to make the first contact as stress-free as possible, both for yourself and the prospect. That way you will be willing to make more calls. You may graduate to a more assertive approach on calls after you have had more experience in qualifying your prospects.

The third component is a clear and short statement of the benefit of your offer. Benefits include things like time saved, cost effectiveness, greater profitability, increased life of equipment, reduced maintenance costs, reduced cost of sales, and so on. The objective is to zero in on how your offer can help solve a problem. While the hook is a sweetener or a risk reducer, the benefit is what will sell your proposition.

The fourth component is a solicitation of interest. Here you are simply asking if the prospect is interested in having more information on your proposal. It is a proposition that is easy to agree to, and sets up a cover for the second call and further development of the relationship. It earns you the right to make the second call. Here you simply say something like: "Would you like to take a look at a report on this fund?" or "Could I send you some information on this?" Some sales professionals feel this type of approach runs the risk of inviting a brush off by prospects who are little more than tire kickers. They readily agree to receive information just as a way to get you off the phone. One way to handle this is to say, "Well, great, Ms. Prospect, I'll be happy to send that along. But before I do, let me ask you a few more questions." And then you can proceed to do more qualifying work.

If you have a well practiced, well-written script, it will serve to ease the way and help you quiet your nervousness. It may sound false to you, but not to the prospect. It is always a good idea to continue on with a script into the next phase of the call, asking qualifying questions. You need to develop the skill of asking searching questions that reveal the situation of the buyer and his or her need for your product or service. This will happen more quickly with a scripted list of questions.

Examples of Good Scripts:

Medical Management Software

Hi! This is _____ with Miller Inc. in Detroit, Michigan.. We specialize in Internet medical management software. I am calling to follow up on a letter our president George Humphries recently sent you regarding his new Internet solution for processing eligibility, claims and referral authorizations.

Did you receive it? Did you have a chance to check out the demo offered at the web site?

For first time clients, we are offering a 20% discount of nearly $5,000 on our new product. It is faster, has more functionality, and costs less than anything currently on the market.

What system do your currently have for processing medical records?

How many physicians are employed at this site?

What platform are you using?

Do you feel your present system is adequate to your needs? Our system is probably two to three times faster than anything on the market today. Would more speed be of interest to you?

Would you be open to learning more about this new Internet based system? Let me have Mr. Humphries give you a call in the next few days to go over some of the details...

Online Job Posting Service

Hello, this is Emma Packard with Jobs and Company, here in the East Bay. We specialize in providing an on line job posting service that has proved to be the quickest, most cost effective way to secure qualified job candidates. Our clients have saved thousands of dollars in advertising costs by using our service and have reduced their time reviewing resumes by x %.

What do you presently do to find and screen candidates?
[Or,] Do you presently use an on line service?
[If not, you probably need to explain to them SUCCINCTLY in one or two sentences how it works. Include BENEFITS!]

May I send you some information about it?

[Close:] I will follow up in a few days to see what you think

Financial Planning

Hi, this is Brian Rogers with _____ here in [name of city.] How are you today? We are a full-service financial planning company specializing in _____ and _____.

The reason for my call is that we are expanding our business in your area and are looking for qualified individuals who are actively in the market. Does this description fit your situation?

Is the current volatility of the market an issue with you? Is this something you would be interested in talking further about with one of our principals?

For first-time clients who act in the next 30 days we are offering a free consultation [$125 value] and assessment of your portfolio… Is this something that would be of interest to you?

[If no:]
We are also offering a financial projection and cash flow analysis, at no charge, for first time clients. This would include discussion of a unique form of hedging that represents one of our specialties. Is this something that you would like to learn more about? If so, I can have one of our principals (mention a name here) contact you and discuss this in greater detail. May I have her give you a call?

[If yes:]

Great, I will have _____ call you in the next day or so to go over some details. Thank you very much for your time.

Software Implementation and Integration Company

Hi, this is _____ with Makeright Consulting in Albany. We are a software implementation and integration company specializing in enterprise and ecommerce applications.

I am calling today because we have a special offer for first time contacts of a two hour, free consultation on your software, hardware and wireless environment.

Are you currently using a legacy system for your enterprise applications or have you updated your business software in HR and Finance?

What initiatives do you have planned in the wireless arena? What about e-procurement? Are there any discussions there about integration of your business systems?

[If positive response in any of above:] May I set up an appointment with one of our contact people in your area?

[Indicate that the free assessment is available if they agree to an appointment. Or go to the next option.]

[If there is resistance on the appointment:] May I have one of our contact people give you a call to follow up and go over some of your options?

[If there is resistance on the phone appointment:] Offer to send collateral about the offerings of the company and that you will be following up.

[If agreement:] Mention the rep's name and secure an agreement for appointment time; or indicate time when he will be calling.

Real Estate Telemarketing Script

Hi, this is _____ with _____ here in [name of city.] The reason I'm calling is we have a listing on _____.[Or:]A house on X St. has just dropped the price and I'm calling to ask if you know of anyone now or in the future interested in moving to this neighborhood.

[Or:]The reason I am calling is that our inventory is down, we have loads of buyers and I calling to ask…as before.

[Or:]The reason I'm calling is we have a young couple interested in moving into the area and_____.

Variations:

This is _____ from _____ Do you have time to help me with a problem? We have a listing at 123 Sycamore and we are trying to find buyers interested in moving to this area. Do you know of anyone now or in the future interested in purchasing a home? How about yourself? Do you have any plans to move in the near future?

[Or:]I am working in this area and I wondered if you know of anyone now or in the future that would be interested in buying or selling their home?"

[Or:]This is _____ with _____, a telemarketing firm in Orinda. The reason I'm calling is that there is a shortage of home buyers right now in your area and I'm wondering if you know of anyone who is looking for a place now or in the future?

Reduce Stress by Changing Your Attitude

Another way to reduce your nervousness in the first fifteen seconds of the call is to adjust your attitude. Inside business development calls (the preferred label for telemarketing calls in corporate America) have become a normal part of the marketing mix employed by American businesses today. The value of goods and services sold over the phone has grown significantly in the last decade, measuring in the hundreds of billions of dollars per year. Projections from the U.S. Commerce Department were that there would be an additional 4.6 million jobs in this field by the end of the 1990's. Business is turning increasingly to the phone to conduct business because of greater cost effectiveness in comparison to a live sales calls. (It has been calculated that it costs a company $10 for a completed call versus $600 to $800 for a face to face sales call). Prospecting by phone is the fastest, least expensive way to reach the greatest number of people over a broad geographical area. And when a phone contact is made in combination with other marketing tactics like direct mail or e-mail, conversion rates are considerably higher. According to Dunn and Bradstreet, phone calls added to direct mail provide two to ten times the leverage over direct mail alone.

You can make many more contacts by phone in an hour of calling than you can out in the field. Of course the rejection rate is higher since your contact rate is so much higher, but there is no question you can talk to more people. Of course, the old timers will tell you that it's much harder for the prospect to say "No" in a face-to-face setting. But I have not found that this outweighs the greater value of a higher contact rate.

What this all means is that calling is and will continue to be an acceptable and normal way of business. There is no reason to feel that you are an "outlaw" for cold calling. It is just a normal part of everyday business. If you think about it that way the calls will be easier for you to make. Our lives, after all, are increasingly a series of networking events or marketing opportunities. If you see calling as an effort to produce your own event, then you are being the architect of others' experience by your behavior. So make it provocative, interesting and fun!

Building Rapport

Many callers feel they need to build "rapport" with the prospect. This is true, but there is a right way and wrong way to do this. Stick to your script and get to the point right away. Don't waste time with insincere questions that can cause you to lose control of the call. However, if it makes you feel comfortable, ask: "How are you today?" or "How are things going?" I have found that it makes no difference in callee acceptance whether you ask this question or not. But it may ease your own comfort level. If possible, in your introduction, mention something you already know about the person, company or location. It can relate either to their business, such as a news item you've seen or a personal relationship you've had before with someone in the company. You can relate to anything you might know about the prospect such as a mutual friend or acquaintance, a shared interest or common membership in a club or association, or a contact at a trade show or mixer. The thing to aim for is any condition, process or affiliation to which you both have a relationship which can then be employed as a building block for creating a relationship.

Using Humor

If you can use tasteful humor, by all means do so. But keep it spontaneous, not scripted. Humor is a great binding agent to our common participation in the human condition; it is a way to convey warmth and conviviality, to show that you are more than a one-dimensional person and it opens the way to a more friendly response. The name of the game is making you and the respondent both feel at ease quickly, so as to build your own confidence level. Your voice quality needs to be free of doubt at the precise moment that you open with your proposal because that is the first impression that sets the stage for what is to follow.

7. The Nuts and Bolts of Telemarketing
Campaigns and Enhancing Call Effectiveness

After I finally overcame my own call avoidance, the next problem was learning to make better calls. For many people, call avoidance is such a big problem that if they can pick up the phone and make the calls at all, it's a major victory! But as you begin to make more and more calls, you will want to improve your conversion rates, so you can make fewer calls but better ones. You'll also want to better leverage your time on the telephone and learn to identify the most responsive prospects. Last but not least, you'll also want to become more relaxed and comfortable on the phone.

Call avoidance and call effectiveness are always yoked together. As you get better on the phone, your avoidance level will decline, and you'll begin to get more and more positive results. In this chapter I will share with you some of the call effectiveness tactics I learned after I mastered call avoidance using the GIRDA formula.

Recently, I had a two-year assignment as a contract telemarketer to a software consulting company specializing in installing business software for large organizations. We called on trade show or conference leads where the prospect had come by our booth and received some information or a free gift. Because of that, there was a high probability that they would recognize the company name, giving us a bit of a head start. The call was already warmed up, and we were hopefully talking to someone who had a reason to be interested in our service. Their response was likely to be friendly or at least businesslike and receptive. If interest was forthcoming, we were to hand off these leads to outside sales reps for follow-up. It is many of the lessons I learned from that experience that I want to share with you now.

Setting up the Campaign

Whether you are setting up a marketing campaign for a new company or starting a new sales job where you must expand your prospect base, the initial task will be to set up a computerized tracking system. This will enable you to track your calls, schedule new ones, note follow-ups and manage the information you will be collecting over the entire prospect relationship. I have used ACT, Goldmine and Siebel as software applications to handle these tasks. For the smaller projects, the first two are more than adequate. These applications permit you to record your calls and all the other things that go with keeping track of your calls and building a valuable source of prospects and clients. But more importantly, as prospects, customers, suppliers and employees all begin to interface by voice, fax, e mail, regular mail, web chat, phone, voice mail and so on, it is critical to capture this data to later be merged into more complex CRM applications (Customer Relationship Management). Even though voice still remains the most natural and powerful of these interfaces, corporate customers will want access to information on a 24/7 basis.

Once you have selected a database management system to track and schedule your calls, you'll need names, addresses and phone numbers of prospects. Forget paper-based lists. It takes a lot of time to enter this data into your computer and can become an excuse for not making calls by justifying the data entry time as "productive" activity. Get the list on disk or from the Internet and import records directly into your database.

When you have your written script prepared, you are ready to begin calling. Once you start dialing, one of the first things that will happen is that you'll find most prospects unavailable. You will be dumped into voice mail. My experience with voice mail is that return calls are rare. I recommend using voice mail as an opportunity to leave a brief message with your name, company name and the nature of your call. I find it helps NOT to expect a call back. But, by leaving the message you have warmed up the call so that when you eventually do connect, they may know something about you. If they recognize your name or voice the next time, you'll be far more comfortable when you do actually talk to them.

Recently, a rookie cold caller contacted me through my web site, www.coldcalling.com and lamented about how many calls it sometimes takes for him to establish contact. I told him that in some respects cold calling is just another job, and like any other job you have to keep at it.

He replied:

Mark, I think you hit the nail on the head by saying "it is just a job." I believe strongly that what we as sales professionals do in our work is listening to all the "I'll think about its," "Send me information," "Fax me your price list," only to have nothing come out of it. Another guy's work is getting filthy dirty, say, working out on a highway construction crew or wherever. A lot of people don't understand the overall game of cold calling and get very frustrated. We have to focus on the fact that people buy for their reasons (not ours) and buy when they are ready and not when we are ready. That's why I am such a strong believer in the pipeline of sales success that says if you requested I send information, I will call you on an every-other-month basis whether you buy or not.

The other day I had a meeting with a guy for whom I had left voice mails about once a month for three YEARS! When I called back, he took my call for the first time and said he wanted to see me today. It looks like he is getting ready to put together a large order with our company. Most people would think it's crazy to follow up for that long with no results. But, I think you just have to sometimes."

Send Me Something!

The issue of "send me something" is an interesting one. Some prospects need the reassurance of a professional looking marketing piece to help convince them that you are a serious player. Others could care less. I don't send the stuff unless it is requested. And some just want to get you off the phone. I put these prospects in one of four categories:

The A category is someone who indicates in my qualification regimen that they will be buying in zero to three months.

B's are for those three to six months out.

D's are for six month follow-up or they are "DEAD."

And, prospects get a C rating if I haven't contacted them yet.

You can classify everyone into one of these categories. The objective with the B's is to move them into the A category. As you personalize your contacts, you can send them different kinds of information or special offers. Some will need lots of contact, in diverse forms, before they become serious prospects, and some will never make it out of the D category. This pipeline will provide you with raw material... those suspects who become prospects and then (hopefully) customers!

How to Further Jumpstart Your Calling Efforts

Here are some ways to enhance your calling performance:

- In telephone work it is critically important to consider what kind of vocal image you project. While your voice is unique to you, it can be adjusted to create the type of impression you want. You can sound more or less interesting, credible or appealing. I am blessed with a deep, sonorous voice that is a definite asset in this line of work. Of course, as a prospector, I don't get to use it much since my conversations are so short! But, I do know that it helps establish credibility. Strength and competence in the voice instills confidence in the mind of the prospect.

• Variety in your voice is key to captivating listeners. You can vary your pitch, rate, tone and volume to create different effects. Melinda Henning in her manual *Doing Business by Phone* (private printing) states that a lower pitch voice is more soothing to the ear and therefore conveys more credibility. She maintains that singing lower and lower notes will expand the lower end of your vocal range. By holding the low sounds as long as you can without forcing them, you will soon be able to use that lower range more readily as you increase your own natural range.

• The average speaking rate is 125 words per minute, about the same as half a page of double-spaced typewritten text. People can listen faster than they can read, so vary your speaking rate to add interest and keep their attention. Maintaining the same rate over time can put your listener into a bored trance. If you tend to speak very quickly, remember to pause occasionally to let listeners assimilate your information. One of my colleagues speaks very quickly, and if you are like me, I'm too polite to ask him to repeat what he just said, so he doesn't get his entire message across.

- Smile first before picking up the phone. Smiling will definitely change the sound of your voice, adding much more personal warmth. It may affect your attitude as well. According to Henning, it takes 33 muscles to frown, but only 13 to smile. Why not take the easy way out? Smiling will help you keep your voice animated, and when you smile, people almost always respond more favorably.

- Set an uninterrupted time aside for making your calls. It's hard to switch back and forth between some other activity and calling. I favor a dedicated time though lately I have been varying my calls with other tasks related to calling to add more interest and variety. But initially, I recommend a single focus.

- I used to believe that once you got through to a prospect, it was necessary to ask the perfunctory "How are you doing today?" question. I regarded this as a useless but necessary bridge to get the conversation rolling. I thought it wasn't really sincere, yet it seemed necessary to initiate the proceedings. Now, I just launch into the dialogue. Prospects seem to be just as cooperative and friendly regardless of whether I use the bridge comment or not. Most prospects just want you to quickly get to the point.

- More often than not the result of a call is that you need to make another call. The prospect isn't there, or even if they do pick up, the conversation may only establish that they are not yet in need of your product or service. You will need to establish what is going to happen next. Be prepared for this and make it part of your script. Be clear why you will be calling again in the future. Perhaps it's because you want to bid on future work, to stay in touch because things change, or because they may grow disenchanted with their present vendor. Other reasons might include an impending event like a seminar or some new offer that may be of interest to the prospect. Whatever the reason, use it to convey to the prospect the impression that you will be calling in the future and that you intend for this relationship to be for the long term. This helps you when you do make that next contact. It will be less stressful because you have already gained "permission" to make the call.

- A laser printer supply broker used to call me once a month to check up on whether I might be needing a new cartridge for my printer. We both knew that at some point I would need her service, that I was not covered by anyone currently, and that she wanted me to think of her when the need arose. The next time I needed a cartridge, she got the order. If she had not kept the name of her company in my memory, I probably would have found a vendor in the yellow pages. But as it was, she got my business because she had become familiar to me. And she had been persistent in trying to secure my business.

- Much of the work of cold calling is to get the ball rolling with new prospects, but in most cases you (or an outside rep) will eventually want to have a face-to-face meeting, assuming the prospect is qualified. The question arises as to whether you want to set this up yourself or hand it over to the rep to make the arrangement. If you use outside reps, I prefer the latter. Let them make the call, explain that they had heard from their business development person that more discussions were appropriate and they want to set an appointment. This is a smoother arrangement in my view and it optimizes the chances for success. These days, a phone appointment can be far easier to secure than a face-to-face meeting. This generally depends on the size and maturity of the organization you are calling. Generally, higher-level managerial and executive types are busy people and harder to book with face-to-face time. They tend to do more work by phone. As a rule, people in smaller companies or those lower on the corporate totem pole tend to be more accessible.

- Never quit dialing because the next contact may be friendly, humorous, forthcoming and a great lead!

- Be proactive in the initial interaction with the screener. If you are asked for information, give it, but always end by asking to speak with the prospect. Keep asking questions.

- Vary your introduction, routine and follow up. Sometimes give name and affiliation, sometimes only your name. Leave voice mail messages one time and don't leave a message the next.

- Vary your prospect lists. Call on one category for a day and then switch to some other group the next.

- Cultivate the screener for cooperative suggestions on alternative ways of gaining access. Success in securing the e-mail address of the prospect is not much of a victory because you lose control and have to follow up with another call. Booking a phone appointment with Mr. Big may be a viable strategy.

- If you are on the line with the screener because your call has not gone through, find out anything you can about the organization so that you can use that information in a later call.

- Be self-disclosing in some of your calls, especially in true cold calls when you have no prior reference or context. Let your true self come out. It helps build rapport. When you don't have a prospect's name, disclosing what you and your company are about is often the only way you can get passed on to the inner sanctum. Such self-disclosure is a must when you are coming in as a complete unknown on a call. Here you must tell the screener, or the prospect, the reason for the call, how you came to have their name and

116

contact details, and why. More is better here because you need to provide lots of reassurance that you are a legitimate, serious, creditable player with a valid offer.

The Second Call

I have come to realize that what is really at stake in prospecting calls is making the second and third and fourth calls to build your database and develop relationships with prospects.

The simplest second call is as a follow-up to collateral that has been sent after the initial call. The focus of the call is to establish your credibility as a vendor, ask further qualifying questions and to close for an appointment if appropriate. What is more likely to happen is that your respondent is going to put you off for one reason or another. That's expected, so make a decision about whether or not you are going to enter this record into your database for future prospecting purposes, and go on to the next call. The second call furthers the relationship building process that begins with the initial contact and goes through several stages:

- Gaining familiarity with the prospect, and vice versa.
- Establishing your competence and reliability as a provider.
- Becoming a partner in a business relationship in which you are providing a value added service or product.

Eventually, a substantial number of your calls will be follow up calls rather than new calls. The calls are made to keep you or your company's name in front of qualified prospects, to ensure that you keep track of changing needs and opportunities and to learn what other departments or other associates of your prospect may have a need for your product or service. Sometimes I have had to spend up to a year of calling before getting to that magic moment when the prospect recognizes my name with a slightly warm and friendly response, "Yes Mark," when I call. It is a small moment but a valued one.

I have also had the experience of calling and calling, getting nowhere with a prospect, being unable to reach him, leaving messages, talking only a few times and getting firmly rebuffed each time, and then have the prospect turn around and buy because something has come up that has suddenly created an urgent need for what I had to offer. I once made 30 calls over a 16-month period to a prospect, talked to him twice in all those attempts, got turned down each time, and then he turned around and made a buying decision in our favor. I had left messages in all that time that helped to establish my company as a player and proved in his mind that we were interested in his business. We got the sale. The lesson here is to KEEP CALLING!

Warming up a Cold Call

I am tempted to say there is no such thing as warming up a call until you have established a relationship with the prospect. However, there are some ways to subtly make the interchange more comfortable, both for yourself and your prospect. Building rapport over the phone is a little like trying to befriend a prickly possum. You don't want to be too friendly and you don't want to be too coldly businesslike either. The right approach combines respect and reaching for a tie that binds whether it is geographic, social, humorous, a previous contact or a newsworthy event pertinent to the prospect's company or industry.

I always identify where I am calling from on the off chance that the prospect has a connection with my location, either in fact or in his imagination. Since I live in the San Francisco Bay Area, on nationwide calls I always mention that I am calling from San Francisco. I hope there is a favorable association with this city or region.

If I don't know anything about the prospect or his company, I ask tactfully if this is a good time to talk. This appeals to a common universe of etiquette. It's a way to show concern for the prospect's time and activity. But watch out for insincerity and be sure that you are not just handing out a ready excuse to get yourself off the phone. I generally find that someone will tell me if it is truly a bad time. (I am always amazed when people pick up the phone only to tell me they are in a meeting!) Of course, they may be in a meeting, but more likely it's an excuse not to deal with a vendor.

Make a humorous comment if the opportunity presents itself. Humor is a great binder. I find this works best if it just comes up in the natural exchange and is not forced. It's part of a more general rule to try and be your natural self on the phone. I know this is hard when you are first battling call avoidance and have all sorts of negative, fear inducing beliefs about how your call is being received. But as time goes on, it is wise for several reasons to let more of your self be engaged. If you are doing a heavy barrage of calls, it helps to keep things interesting and challenging. It reduces your own stress level and it makes you a more interesting communicator. After all, this is a human interchange, and it enhances the dialogue if you permit "arrivals" in your consciousness to flow into your talk such as an aside, an observation, or a reference to what is happening in your environment. Again, let prudence be your guide and don't over do it.

8. Implementation of Strategies

Now that I have presented a formula or regimen for overcoming call avoidance and covered the nuts and bolts of the calling process, are you ready to make some calls? The temptation may still be present to procrastinate and prevaricate and put off indefinitely in a vague hope that something better will come along as a business development strategy.

Watch Out for Unending Rumination

The effect of procrastination or rumination about one's resistance and avoidance in making cold calls is usually just more thinking, more thoughts, loosely chained together, leading to still more thoughts, some of which repeat themselves over time leading to new resolves and new interpretations. I know because this happened to me during the days and months that I engaged in my own avoidance rituals. One is seemingly caught in a circular interpretative web, an endless loop if you like, contemplating the implications of preceding considerations without ever taking any new action. It brings to mind a quote from Saul Bellow: "Our thoughts are like a stationary bicycle; they don't get us anywhere."

These ruminations are a sign, according to psychologists Richard S. Lazarus and Carolyn Aldwin (*Stress and Coping:*

An Integrative Perspective, Guildford Press, 1999), that you are protecting yourself against some threat, some form of stress, in this case the imagined threat that you will be treated rudely or that an impending event such as the response of the prospect will be negative and painful, and you believe you won't be able to handle it.

Rumination is assumed to persist until the individual either satisfies the frustrated goal or disengages from the goal altogether as you would if you gave up calling and decided to concentrate on other, less stressful forms of business development like direct mail or advertising in the mass media. I myself have had extensive experience with this sort of thing and have come to believe that this rumination **is** endless, fruitless and functions primarily as a defense against calling. It's hard to give up because it's so comforting. You spend all this time trying to figure out your own avoidance, or how you can get leads without making cold calls, only to discover that it isn't a problem that can be solved inwardly via more introspection but only in interchanges with the outside world. The puzzle of the blockage can only be resolved by interacting with the world until the erroneous assumptions are proved false and your behavior is freed up to serve your own agenda. Even then, the impediment to calling is still there but you have made progress because now you know that it is manageable. This is a far better resolution than what happens for many others who give up too soon guaranteeing failure. I used to tell my seminar attendees: "Now don't go out and make a bunch of calls and then stop because you don't get any results. Don't stop too soon." One of my current clients reported that he makes five attempts to reach a prospect and only if those five fail does he go on to the next prospect. In my current calling work, I average 10 calls just to reach a prospect! It's easy to give up too soon. It's easy but it's self-defeating.

A real estate agent I recently met firmly resists making calls, but sends out lots of marketing pieces. She has disengaged from the goal of making any cold calls, and accordingly is not engaged in ruminations about shortcomings, failure of nerve or lack of courage. She doesn't waste time procrastinating any more about not making cold calls. She has "resolved" the issue in a way that is comforting but still leaves her short of prospects. (These are the folks who are vulnerable to any new, non-cold calling marketing idea that comes along. The latest I have seen is a lottery type contest in which in exchange for giving out your name as someone possibly interested in buying or selling real estate, you gain a chance to win a weekend retreat at a Bed and Breakfast and a special mud bath at a Health Spa.)

Know What Motivates You and What You Believe

Committed callers who want to make progress are faced with implementing the strategies discussed in this book in a continuous and consistent manner. And this comes down to a question of motivation, to knowing why you want what you want and how you are going to go about getting it. In my experience, even when you find answers to these questions, and it may LOOK like they should be a necessary and sufficient cause for implementation, they are not enough to guarantee action. This is particularly the case when facing an activity like cold calling that many feel they need to do but do not WANT to do. This is a crucial distinction. The former conveys obligation and duty; the latter implies desire, hunger, craving and wish, as in "I need to make 30 calls a day, but I want to find referral leads instead"; "I need to make 10 sales presentations, but I want prospects to call ME up to buy my service"; "I need to implement my marketing plan, but I want to concentrate on developing new products." Want implies pleasure, stimulation and ease; need does not necessarily imply this outcome, and often requires stamina or personal discomfort or endurance to realize. Hence with a need, more than motivation is required. You also need self-confidence or self-efficacy, that is, the inspiring belief that you have the power or ability to fulfill the need.

For several years now I have been pursuing the question of what lies at the heart of self-regulation or striving to attain any worthwhile goal. What does it really take to successfully self-regulate fear, doubt, temptation, poor self- esteem or whatever constitutes the inner barrier that prevents intention realization? I have come up with several good candidates that make sense in theory but which never seem to operate on the level of daily experience. Hence, I thought good candidates for the heart of self-regulation were such things as responsibility to yourself, especially, or to some group whose opinion matters. I like the argument of existentialists that since you are the one who must create your destiny, then only you have the responsibility to carry out the actions necessary to realize that destiny. Other candidates for what it takes to be a disciplined striver include role models (others who have gone before you and achieved significant outcomes), positive expectations (also known as the power of positive thinking), and accountability partners who help you stay focused and to whom you report your progress.

It certainly makes sense to believe that for effective self-regulation to take place you need a strong motivator. I believe that the best candidate for the heart of self-regulation is a powerful driver that mobilizes you to action, whether it's satisfying the needs of others, fulfilling your own dreams or the attainment of some special material or psychological reward. Finally, I remain convinced that a strong belief in the reliability and validity of your vehicle is also a sound basis for effective self-regulation. This is a close cousin of self-regulation, the belief that "you can do it," or self-efficacy.

Want It, Need It and Know You *Will* Get It

Self-efficacy often comes about when people acquire an internal control orientation that leads them to set goals and develop generally successful means of attaining them. It is a belief that one can perform adequately in a given situation and realize one's goal. Conversely, we tend to not try things we don't believe we can do. We avoid performances when we think we are not adequate, or don't have what it takes, to be successful. Even when we have the desire and the ability, we may not take required action if we think we lack what it takes to respond to a specific situation or undertake a certain activity. It all depends on how we evaluate ourselves, on how we think about our desires and abilities to fulfill them. Which is to say it all comes down to a question of belief in ourselves and in the means we use to attain goals.

I have struggled for years to uncover what really inspires and motivates me. I formulated many compelling reasons and justifications to provide a foundation for expressing myself in the world and seeking to fulfill my ideals. But even so there was often a lingering avoidance to really commit and I now conclude it is because of lack of belief in my own conclusions.

In the cold calling example, many are defeated by an attitude of low self- efficacy; they don't see immediate results, so they quit. Or they don't **think** they can be assertive enough to succeed at cold call selling, so they give up; or they **think** they won't be hardy enough to endure all the rejection so they surrender to the belief that it won't work for them. Or, they **think** it's futile to call because they won't be effective, so they don't try.

I recall that in my own early cold calling days, progress was fitful and sometimes non-existent as I was not convinced that cold calling worked, or that I could make it work. All I had was an uncomfortable feeling when I made the calls. It is very hard to move ahead when you don't expect success. Futility is a difficult competitor. There were many days when it seemed that more calls only meant more rejection. But as time wore on and I kept at it, little by little I began to see results. The results gave me a little confidence, enough to keep going and try again. All it took was a start. If I had held to my early beliefs that it couldn't work then I would have probably given up. But I was willing to keep trying on the assumption that given a little persistence, any skill can be learned, if not mastered.

Expectations Create their Own Results

Expectations of success or failure can change in light of feedback from performance but they are more likely to create the predicted feedback and this becomes a self-fulfilling prophecy. In my experience, the twin factors of feeling that one is not good enough and fear of disapproval by the prospect create an underlying sense of low self-efficacy and low self-confidence that bring cold prospecting activity quickly to a halt. In fact, as I discovered, they bring to a halt just about any initiative that you try. One is made to feel inferior by being put in a down power position via placement in the role of supplicant or "mere" solicitor; and one rightly fears that the chances of success are remote; the resulting expectations are low that good things will happen. It's as if the activity itself produces, by its feedback, the feeling of inferiority and reinforces the fear of disapproval since rejection is so common. This produces what I call the "telemarketer's lament," which is that most of the time your efforts seemingly end in naught; only rarely do good things happen so that you feel vindicated in your efforts. And, assuming that the monetary reward is sufficient, and subject to enhancement as you get better, then the lament becomes at least endurable.

Hence, now to be told that one can learn to make cold calls by goal setting, incrementally increasing the goals, record keeping, and accountability--the GIRDA formula--arouses resistance because the nature of the activity continues to be aversive, unless one can find a way to reframe its meaning so that implementation of these strategies is done on a consistent basis.

Perspectives That Favor Implementation

The mindsets necessary to achieve successful self-regulation as this pertains to cold calling are as follows:

- The first element is to have a clear objective or goal that is served by your cold calling marketing efforts. A clear goal provides the underlying legitimacy for your calling and answers the why question behind what you are doing. As Walker suggests, (Sidney Walker, *Trusting Yourself*, High Plains Publishing Co., 1988) a goal is something that is tangible and measurable in terms of quantity and time. If your goal is to talk to fifty prospects a week, taking a specific amount of time, you will know with certainty if you have met your goal.

- A vision, which provides the context and meaning for a goal, can be a single picture in your mind or it can be a series of mental images, like a movie. It can cover any amount of time. The most powerful visions are the ones that appeal to as many of the five senses (seeing, feeling, hearing, taste and smell) as possible. It is easier to achieve a goal if you can both clearly see and deeply feel its importance, says Walker. Walker advises that once you have a clear vision of what you want to achieve, use as many of your senses as possible to set or formulate this vision in your mind. Then check to make sure your vision feels intuitively right.

Believe in Your Vision

You give your vision the energy it needs to become real by BELIEVING in it. As Walker argues, believing is a combination of imagining your vision as possible (self-efficacy again) that is, as subject to being effectively realized by yourself, and staying in touch with the feeling of what it would be like to have your vision be real.

My experience with using a constructed vision or generalized end as a guide to everyday activities is that it is hard to keep it in awareness in moment-to-moment activities. One can formulate a compelling version of some future state that one would like to enact or bring to completion. While this helps provide an underlying justification, unless it is kept in awareness its impact is minimal as a driving force in sustaining momentum in day-to-day activities.

As I have indicated, I have entertained numerous candidates for self-motivation that I thought might provide the energy and commitment to drive me forward. But the fate of these attempts has always been short lived.

For a time I thought that a contract was an essential ingredient to self- regulation, to sustain discipline and determination. Yet contracts seem to always terminate through neglect, or they can be weaseled out of with your accountability partner because of lack of enforceability. At other times I have thought that surrendering to the demands of discipline-- and cold calling is certainty a discipline-- was the key, but this turned out to be a mere intellectual construct. Guilt or an urgent financial need or moral passion have also arisen as possible motivators, but none seem to work over the long term.

Progression and Regression

My conclusion is that both progression and regression are the normal part of striving and struggling to implement a program of cold calling, or any serious intention for that matter. Some days you move vigorously forward with new behaviors and accomplishments; but other times you turn inward to experience and deal with the fears and doubts and dysfunctional patterns that come up as a result of moving ahead into new territory. These elements need to be processed in interaction with one's spouse, business partner, therapist or other close confidant who can provide reassurance and validation, at least for the occasional episodes of progress.

But while progression and regression may empirically more accurately describe the process of striving, implicit in this statement is the understanding and faith that, at bottom, the means used are both valid and efficacious. You need to be convinced in your own mind that the behavioral strategies for overcoming call avoidance I have recommended will indeed work; that daily goal setting, incrementally increasing goals at your own pace, and recording the fate of your calls-- the GIRDA formula-- will work to enable you to make the calls.

The evidence for this proposition is threefold: (1) Of the more than 500 sales professionals and entrepreneurs who have taken my seminars, 75% report an increase in their calling rate as a result of using these methods. (2) My own calling rate continues to be sustained at a high rate even after several years of calling. (3) The principle of progressive desensitization which underlies the behavioral component of the recommended solution is well established in psychology. A recent book by Martin Seligman (*Learned Optimism,* Pocket Books, 1998) indicates that of the methods for behavior change available, those using progressive desensitization tend to produce more positive results than many other methods.

Control Mastery Theory

In this process of accepting both progression and regression, what comes up are the unconscious negative beliefs that tend to block forward movement toward your goals. It may take a long time for you to discover what particular beliefs, unknown to you, are holding you back. Most often our difficulties, according to psychotherapy, are caused by unconscious shame, unconscious fears and unconscious guilt. Whatever the case, I find myself in agreement with Control Mastery theory in psychotherapy that asserts that the only sure way to cope with these "grim" beliefs is to interact with the real world and get some feedback as to the veracity of these beliefs. According to Control Mastery theory, many of our adult patterns of avoidance are a result of early traumas that give rise to unconscious beliefs that a similar situation may bring forth similar threats in adulthood. For instance, if we were shouted at and berated for initiating new lines of action as a child, we are likely to unconsciously believe the same thing will happen as an adult, and most certainly will when we go to make cold calls. Hence, to avoid the reenactment of this same scene, we avoid initiating new contacts for fear the same thing will happen. This is an unconscious belief and until it can be made conscious, it cannot be controlled. But it is control of these mistaken beliefs that is the essence of overcoming call avoidance. And this is achieved mainly by the application of the behavioral and cognitive techniques I have outlined.

Take the Leap

We are brought full circle: to implement the behavioral regimens recommended here calls for goals and a sense of vision; but striving for these ends is undermined by negative, unconscious beliefs. The only effective way to deal with these beliefs is to test them in the real world, which brings us right back to the beginning step or the LEAP. The LEAP is the moment when one decides to stop speculating and start acting, rather than attempting to draw out the consequences of preceding considerations as in the rumination defense.

The leap is when you take an action in behalf of your sales proposition. In the context of cold calling, it's when you write a letter or e-mail to ease the way for a call, or get together a list of prospect names and telephone numbers preparatory to a session of calling. Or it could be the action of going to an event, trade show or networking meeting at which you harvest a cluster of contact names or business cards that then become your starting list to call. Or perhaps the action you need to take is to formulate a script to ease the way in making your calls so that you can begin to put together the numbers of calls that will eventually begin to lead to new business.

Whatever you choose, these are some of the actions you need to take to get started. The time eventually arrives when you have to do the acts rather than make the arguments. You have to move into your experience rather than continue to dwell in your reasons and you have to actualize instead of intellectualize.

Fortunately, it can happen and has for many. So good luck and good calling!

9. Interview With a Champion Cold Caller

The following interview was conducted with a financial planner and stockbroker who works for one of the major brokerage houses in California. She is very successful in her cold calling work. She consistently rates as one of the top five producers in her office year after year. I first met her when she came to one of my seminars to perfect her skills. This woman, whom I shall call Maggie, is 39 years old, married, with no children. She embodies both a high motivation to achieve and a solid belief in her own capabilities.

Many people in your position don't like cold calling, what's your secret?

I think cold calling is really fun. Cold calling is one way that you can reach out to a huge number of people, quickly. My anchor in the activity is when I can get the person on the other end of the line to truly connect with me. I like it because it's an opportunity to connect with people and to touch their lives that I wouldn't touch during the course of a normal business day. I don't mind wading through the people who don't want to talk because I find that very few are truly rude. They really are willing to say yes or no, or I'd rather not talk about it, or this isn't a good time, or whatever their response may be. My preference is that they let me know right away.

Can you give an example of how you approach someone on the phone?

One of the things I call on is the seminar. I say, "Hi, this is _____ with _____. I'm going to be giving a seminar on Investing 101-- Fundamentals of Investing. I wondered if you'd be interested in coming?" And they are going to say: "yes" or "no"; "I've got a broker"; "I'm too busy to talk to you right now"; "Call me back"; "No I'm not interested"; or "Can you send me some info on that?"

If I am cold calling on individuals at a residence, there are peak times when it is better to call. The best time to call is 9:00 to 11:30 Saturday morning. You'll find a higher success ratio during that time than any other time. The other time that is great is 6:00 to 8:00 p.m. at night. And the other time that I like to call is any weekday morning between 9:00 and 11:30 am. This is the time when I will get retirees at home. That's all there is to it!

How do you handle the issue of disrupting dinner, or when it isn't a good time?

I say: "Great, when is a good time to call? I appreciate your being candid with me, what's a better time for you? Is it later, is it earlier, would you prefer if I call during business hours?" So you immediately ask another question just to engage. And I have had people who said: "We're just sitting down to dinner, this isn't a good time." But, I know they wouldn't answer that way if they weren't interested, so then I know I've got at least a chance, so that's a reasonable call back.

When they say this isn't a good time, do you feel you're intruding?

I feel that the services I am offering my clients are superior. I'll say: "When is a good time for you. Is evening or morning better?"

If they say, "Call me in a couple of weeks in the morning," what do you say?

I say, "How early in the morning would you like me to call?" If they say call back in a couple of weeks, I usually call back in a week, because they will forget in a couple of weeks.

What do you do to help build your relationship with prospects?

If someone says call back in a week, I send them a copy of my newsletter along with a note saying that I will be talking with them in a week. The next time I call, they will have some information about me, and about how I run my business. From the newsletter they will also know something more about investing than they probably knew before. Maybe they tossed it, but maybe before they did, they at least saw my photograph, so my next call will be warmer.

They very rarely will hang up on me. Sometimes they honestly say, "I've got a broker, I've been working with her for 15 years." End of subject. And that's OK too.

Are you warming up calls with mailouts? And if so, do you anticipate a warmer response because they know a little bit more about you?

I do use mailouts. There's no doubt that the response I get back from those type of warmer phone calls reflects a much higher level of at least listening or connecting with me. My goal on the first or second call is to get an appointment. And if I get an appointment on the first phone contact, absolutely I will close him or her because that's somebody who is truly committed to listening, and committed to doing some kind of financial planning.

Who are your prospects? Are you calling on mostly retirees, business owners or what?

It depends. Sometimes I will use the reverse directory and because I know this area so well, I'm looking at where the larger homes are, where more money resides. At other times it's not always the largest homes, but it is the nice neighborhood that's been established for a long time and those people have more disposable income to do investing.

I'm intrigued with your attitude towards calling. It seems like it is an adventure for you and that you know that you are going to be successful in the long run. Is that true?

I probably have a very unique viewpoint in terms of making cold calls. I met my best friend through a cold call. And it is very rare that you'll hear someone say that. After she and I connected on the phone, we made an appointment for a couple of days later. When I met her for the first time, we absolutely connected from that moment forward. After she became a client of mine for a year and a half, we just became incredible friends over time.

Has that new found friendship influenced your subsequent calls?

Sure. I know that another great friend could be out there! Maybe not another best friend, but a client to whom I can truly bring value. I believe each of us knows what their ultimate driver is. For me it's knowing that I am creating value for my clients.

If you believe you will be able to help them in some significant way, the fact that they are now strangers doesn't really make much difference, does it?

No, it doesn't. In fact, there's something about being able to reach out and literally touch somebody's life in a fundamental way that is very satisfying. You start out with nothing, not knowing them at all, and then bring them into your life as a successful client.

I'll give you an example. A woman who got put in my list just by happenstance called me. Usually prospects never contact me just from a mailer. But she contacted me. She knew she needed to do something and she wasn't even in my life a week before. I was able to make a difference for her.

Could you tell me more stories of good things that happened through cold calling?

One woman I cold called made an appointment with me on the first call. She was willing to sit down with me and discuss what she was doing with her finances. Usually I look for people in transition, where something major has happened in their life like a job change, divorce, or relocation. This woman was a bit different. It turned out her son had AIDS, and she was looking to set up some educational funding for her grandchildren, and she wanted to control those funds. She wanted a line of succession should anything happen to her before her son died. Some time after I helped her set up that transition, I also helped her through the loss of her son.

Another woman who made an appointment with me had a husband who was in the hospital dying of cancer. She was walking around with a binder that literally had hundreds of thousands of dollars in stock certificates and did not understand what she had. Her husband had been doing all the finances. I was able to get it all registered in her name so that upon his death it was all taken care of. So at the point when she is in the most grief, she will know that she and her daughter will be well taken care of. I'm not shy about calling people that I might be able to someday help in a similar way.

You have undoubtedly enjoyed the benefits of a huge bull market the last few years. Now that the returns are not so great, isn't it going to be much more difficult to make the calls for fear of rejection?

In my business, brokers hate to call when the market is down or when it's a bad news day. But I can tell you that I brought in my largest client by calling on bad news! I had the guts to call and say: "It's my understanding that you are in XYZ stock, and by the way it's down seven points and I just wanted to let you know, its still a good company, and it's going to be fine. Hang with the stock, the profits are there, their product is there, all of the things that you brought the company for are still there, so don't worry, even if you are in this position, I believe that things will work out." They called me back the next day and said, "Our regular broker didn't even call us, and you know what? We really need to start doing business with you."

Why is this a tougher call, the call to a prospect in a down market?

It is tougher, but the reality is you really need to be with your clients and prospects much more when there's bad news than when there is good news. I think the fear is that you will be associated with the down-trend, but their own broker is not calling them on those days, so it leaves the door wide open for you. I've even had one of my clients say, "You know, you always call when its a down market."And I responded, "Yes I do, because the reality is that the tough times are when you need me the most. When things are going great you don't need me holding your hand!"

When you are doing a cold calling campaign during your active calling time, how many calls do you make on a daily basis?

During peak calling periods, my goal is 200 dials a day, but I never hit that. It's very hard to come even close to that unless you don't take any incoming calls and block out your time. My biggest day was about 175 dials, which for me is about six hours of calling, three in the morning and three in the afternoon.

So how many contacts can you realistically make in an hour?

It depends on the numbers of connects. Out of one hundred phone calls, I get ten that connect fairly well. From the ten I usually get three that could be considered really good prospects and I then would get one or two clients out of those three. If I can get in front of a client, my close ratio is probably in the 90 percent range. So, my goal on every call is always to get an appointment. Over time, this amounts to about one client for three and a half hours of calling.

How much income do you make for each hour of cold calling?

It's hard for me to figure what the income is for one client from four or five hours of calling because you can have a client for a number of years with a large or small portfolio. I've found that they are either ready to make an appointment, or not, within two to three calls. If they don't set a time by then, it isn't going to happen for me.

But the industry standard is more like six or seven calls until they agree to an appointment, isn't it?

Yes, statistically they say the biggest return is on the sixth to seventh phone call. But it doesn't seem to matter if I go beyond the third call. If I don't have an appointment by then, I can call them until the cows come home and it won't matter.

How do you engage your prospects?

My goal is to have the client talking within 15 seconds of a connection. I try to get three yes's very quickly. I'll ask something like: "Are you currently receiving any tax free income?" They're going to say: "Tax-free income? What do you mean? What are you talking about?" Now I've got her talking. I respond with: "That's income that you don't have to worry about the government taking their bite out; it comes straight to you." If she says, "I do have some of that." I've got one yes already! Then I'll follow with: "Would you be willing to listen to a good idea about municipal bonds?" And if she says: "Yes." I follow by asking: "What kinds of things do you currently buy so I can send you some information?" Now I'm into fact finding, but I'm letting them talk much more than I talk. People like to be listened to.

How long have you been doing this and do you still enjoy it?

I've been doing it for three years now. The two clients I opened last week were $100,000 each and above. I can truly say I enjoyed that!

If you were going to advise someone new to sales, or someone just trying to grow their business, how would you help and encourage them to make cold calls?

I would say, set a specific time each day that you are going to do it, and make sure you stick to that time. That time may be only fifteen minutes long, but it's OK. Then have something around you that is part of a comfort zone for you, whatever that is, a certain chair, a certain desk, a special cup of coffee… something you like. I happen to like to write with green pens because they remind me of money. I also like to have a canary tablet even though I have a computer database. For me, there is nothing like physically writing as someone is telling me something!

Do you find your connect ratio goes up as your skills improve?

For me, it comes in waves. I may make thirty dials and not even connect once and then boom, within ten more calls, I will have connected eight times! It's not a straight line that for every ten calls you'll make one connect. Rather, it seems to come in waves. When you are really on your stuff, you really connect a lot. It seems like when you are really relaxed, the prospects hear it in your voice.

I understand that you once took a voice class?

A long time ago (I'll credit Tony Robbins), I learned that 55% of your communication is physiology, 37% is your voice and tone cues, and only 7% is in the words. So early on I learned it really didn't matter a hill of beans what I said. It mattered how I said it, how I held my body and how I projected the tone of my voice. A friend and I used to work for a major corporation. Our voices, for whatever reason, used to turn off the company voice mail system. We learned to lower our tone to get our messages across to each other without getting cut off and having to redial. That was a valuable lesson. In fact, after that I went and took a class in voice power. Some people already have a deep voice to begin with, but when I started out, the more excited I got, the higher my voice went! I had to work at bringing my tone down and slowing myself down. Most salespeople are visual, speak very quickly, and want to make their point very quickly. Most buyers are kinesthetic and they talk more slowly. The people in the middle are what we call auditories and they actually only comprise 25% of the population. Because of that, I've learned to use words that are visual. I'll ask, "Can you see what I mean?" "Can you hear what I am saying?" or "How does that feel to you?" Each of those questions is geared towards a specific type of client.

One more thing along that same subject. As prospects speak to me, I use their own words back to them, words that make sense to them. Also, if you speak at the same pace and tone as someone it's a way to connect with them. If I get someone on the phone that talks fast, I'll talk fast back to them.

Have you ever practiced on audiotape?

Yes, in that training in the "board room" I mentioned. They recorded us and we heard ourselves played back. It was ok, but it's not something I have done a lot of although I'm sure that for some people that's a good practice. I tend to be more visual, so one of the things that has been very helpful for me is writing scripts for myself. With a script I know exactly what I will say to the prospect. I also list the five or six biggest objections and my responses to them. I did it on large index cards. I printed big so I could read them easily, and put them across the top of my desk.

One final question… how would you advise someone who has just made 40 calls and got zip, zero results in return?

When I first made calls in the brokerage industry, they had a "board room" where sixty of us at a time had to make cold calls. When we finished, this guy said, "That was awful, and really hard!" I turned to him and said, "You know what, digging ditches is hard, cleaning sewers is hard, picking up garbage is really hard, but picking up a wonderful, clean, pretty telephone where I get to punch little numbers, is not hard! All we're doing is playing a numbers game. That's all it is. And at the end of that numbers game there's someone out there who really wants and needs your services. Just keep calling because it works!

For More Information:

Sanford Associates offers a number of products and services designed to help you overcome sales call avoidance and be more effective on the phone:

Free Newsletter—
To subscribe to Mark's free weekly Telephone Prospecting Tips Newsletter log on to www.coldcalling.com

Helpful Products—
• Taking the Cold Sweats Out of Cold Calling
• How to Create Winning Telemarketing Scripts

For more information on these and other products please go to www.coldcalling.com or call toll free 1 (866) 826-5322

Services—
• Script Consultations
• One-on-One Consulting Services
• On Site Seminars and Workshops
• Cyber Seminars

To contact Dr. Sanford email him at msanford@coldcalling.com or call toll free 1 (866) 826-5322

www.coldcalling.com